Improving the U.S. Military's Understanding of Unstable Environments Vulnerable to Violent Extremist Groups

Insights from Social Science

David E. Thaler, Ryan Andrew Brown, Gabriella C. Gonzalez,
Blake W. Mobley, Parisa Roshan

Prepared for the United States Army

The research described in this report was sponsored by the United States Army under Contract No. W74V8H-06-C-0001.

Library of Congress Cataloging-in-Publication Data is available for this publication.

ISBN 978-0-8330-8164-3

The RAND Corporation is a nonprofit institution that helps improve policy and decisionmaking through research and analysis. RAND's publications do not necessarily reflect the opinions of its research clients and sponsors.

Support RAND—make a tax-deductible charitable contribution at www.rand.org/giving/contribute.html

RAND® is a registered trademark.

RAND OFFICES
SANTA MONICA, CA • WASHINGTON, DC
PITTSBURGH, PA • NEW ORLEANS, LA • JACKSON, MS • BOSTON, MA
DOHA, QA • CAMBRIDGE, UK • BRUSSELS, BE
www.rand.org

Preface

This report documents the results of a study commissioned by the U.S. Army entitled "Improving Understanding of the Environment of Irregular Warfare." The objective of the study was to help defense analysts identify and assess key factors that create and perpetuate such an environment to enable them to inform military decisions on resource allocation. The motivation for the study was a concern by the analytic community that the wargames and models they use to provide insights to commanders and policymakers on irregular warfare (IW) retained underlying assumptions about the surrounding environments that were not well-enough informed or corroborated by important bodies of research outside the military. The present study's task was to survey theories, schools of thought, and existing models in the areas of anthropology, sociology, and related social sciences that could be useful to the U.S. Army in providing insights into the environments in which insurgency, terrorism, and other extremist violence and instability may arise. Based on the survey and a set of focused discussions with sociologists, anthropologists, and political scientists who have experience with IW and social science theory, RAND researchers identified and examined 12 key factors giving rise to these environments and then discerned areas of consensus among social scientists regarding the salience of these factors. The research team also identified qualitative and quantitative metrics that could be used to analyze environments in which the factors may play a role.

The findings of this study should be of interest to defense analysts seeking scientifically grounded insights into causes and perpetuators of unstable environments in which violent extremist groups can arise and thrive.

This research was sponsored by the Director of the Center for Army Analysis and conducted within RAND Arroyo Center's Strategy, Doctrine, and Resources Program. RAND Arroyo Center, part of the RAND Corporation, is a federally funded research and development center sponsored by the United States Army.

The Project Unique Identification Code (PUIC) for the project that produced this document is HQD105742.

For more information on RAND Arroyo Center, contact the Director of Operations (310-393-0411, ext. 6419; fax: 310-451-6952; Marcy_Agmon@rand.org) or visit Arroyo's website at http://www.rand.org/ard.html.

Abstract

Over the previous decade, operations associated with irregular warfare (IW) have placed large demands on U.S. ground forces and have led to development of new Army and Joint doctrine. This report helps analysts identify and assess key factors that create and perpetuate environments susceptible to insurgency, terrorism, and other extremist violence and instability to inform military decisions on allocation of analytic and security assistance resources. The report focuses in particular on sources of understanding about these environments from the fields of sociology and cultural anthropology. RAND researchers surveyed existing sociological and anthropological theories and schools of thought and identified 12 key factors that give rise to and sustain unstable environments. The research found a relatively high degree of consensus among experts regarding the salience of these factors. The factors are interrelated and mutually dependent in complex ways. The report proposes a series of qualitative and quantitative metrics for each of the 12 factors and uses them in an analytic construct for assessing countries and regions based on their susceptibility to unstable environments.

Contents

Figures

Tables

Box

Summary

The 2012 strategic guidance of the U.S. Department of Defense affirms counterterrorism and irregular warfare (IW) as a primary mission of the U.S. armed forces.[1] Over more than a decade, this mission has placed large and new demands on U.S. ground forces. The current thinking reflected in the new guidance holds that these ground forces should emphasize non-kinetic operations intended to persuade the population in areas affected or threatened by violent extremist groups to cooperate with the United States and its local partners in order to counter and resist the activities of those groups. Engagement with partners to prevent conflict before it occurs—"Phase 0" operations—minimizes both cost and the need for intervention with U.S. ground forces. However, little consensus exists on why the conditions that require such operations emerge, creating uncertainty as to the actions needed to mitigate conditions in which violent extremist groups emerge, survive, and thrive.

This report sheds light on conditions that give rise to and sustain environments that are susceptible to insurgency, terrorism, and other extremist violence and instability. The objective of the report is to help defense analysts identify and assess key factors that create and perpetuate such environments to enable them to inform military decisions on allocating resources globally across areas of instability and within nations encountering instability. The report focuses in particular on sources of understanding about environments vulnerable to extremist violence from the fields of sociology, cultural anthropology, and related social sciences. The research team surveyed existing sociological and anthropological theories and schools of thought as to the main sources of instability that could give rise to local instability. From this review, we identified key relevant factors and then discerned areas of consensus among social scientists regarding the salience of these factors through focused discussions with experts. Finally, we identified qualitative and quantitative metrics that could be used in analysis of environments in which these factors may play a role. We also used an analytic framework to demonstrate how analysts might apply the factors, using two historical cases (the Shining Path in Peru and the Maoist Insurgency in Nepal) as examples.

Twelve factors emerged from the research:

- the level of ***external support*** for violent extremist groups
- the extent to which the ***government is considered illegitimate or ineffective*** by the population

---

[1] U.S. Department of Defense, *Sustaining U.S. Global Leadership: Priorities for 21st Century Defense*, Washington, D.C., January 2012.

- the presence of tribal or ethnic indigenous populations with a ***history of resisting state rule*** and/or cultures that encourage or justify violent behavior
- the levels of ***poverty and inequality*** or the presence of one or more groups that have recently lost status or power
- the extent to which ***local governance is fragmented, weak, or vulnerable*** to replacement or co-option by nonstate group institutions
- the existence of ***ungoverned space***
- the presence of ***multiple violent, nonstate groups competing for power***
- ***the level of government restriction on political or ideological dissent*** and the extent to which individuals feel alienated from the governing process
- ***the level of consistency and/or agreement*** between a violent extremist group's goals and philosophy and the preferences, worldview, and ideology of target populations
- the extent to which population and extremist ***groups perceive faltering government commitment*** to a counterinsurgency (COIN) campaign
- ***the capacity, resources, and expertise of violent extremist groups***
- the pervasiveness of ***social networks*** capable of being galvanized and mobilized to resistant action.

Key Findings

The following findings emerged from our research:

- While U.S. military doctrine espouses a number of root causes and perpetuators of environments in which IW is engaged, it does not offer critical analysis of the concepts. Moreover, there are significant commonalities among U.S. doctrinal publications on trends and triggers associated with such conflicts. However, military doctrine does not acknowledge that uncertainty exists among social scientists about the salience of some of these causes in general as well as in specific conflicts.
- Sociology, anthropology, and related fields offer insights into instigators and perpetuators of environments vulnerable to insurgencies and terrorism. The application of sociological and anthropological theories to the study of these environments can shed light on the interplay between individuals' personal inclinations, beliefs, or position in a society and the political, economic, and organizational structures in which they are situated.
- We discerned 12 underlying factors relevant to unstable environments prone to violent extremism from anthropology, sociology, political science, and related fields. These were validated through a combination of literature review, comparison with detailed COIN case studies, and focused discussions with social scientists.
- Agreement in the literature and among experts regarding the salience of these factors generally is high. Disagreement tended to center on the degree to which the factors are universally applicable and the relative importance of certain subfactors.
- Factors are linked to one another through complex, mutually dependent interrelationships. There are multiple feedback loops in which each factor strengthens or exacerbates others over time in a given conflict. Where these interrelationships can be disrupted, individual factors can be weakened as sources of instability or sustainment of violence.

- Qualitative and quantitative metrics can be developed that enable assessment and tracking of factors. There are a number of relevant metrics in the public domain that are updated annually and can be easily accessed for analysis.
- Metrics can be used in a scheme for assessing and prioritizing countries and regions based on the presence of factors that could give rise to unstable environments. Such a scheme could help U.S. planners and analysts focus level of effort and identify priorities for resource allocation globally across regions that are susceptible to violence and instability.

Recommendations

We recommend that the U.S. Army analytic community take the following actions:

- ***Incorporate factors and associated metrics into IW-related analytic games and models.*** Supplement existing tools with components that enable consideration of the relative strength of factors in particular scenarios and encourage concepts for mitigating negative effects on the fight.
- ***Evaluate levels of potential instability and extremist violence using the assessment scheme outlined in this report.*** Analysts can track trends in factor prevalence in particular countries or regions to alert decisionmakers to growing areas of instability or to follow the consequences of U.S. or local government action.
- ***Conduct research to probe and map overlays and interrelationships among factors in specific cases.*** Such research would indicate where overlays exist and how factors interact with each other. Research on Iraq and Afghanistan, two environments with which U.S. analysts are intimately familiar and where understanding is relatively fresh, should be considered.
- ***Develop a prioritization approach based on the factors and assessment scheme that helps indicate where best to allocate analytic and security-assistance resources.*** Analysts may use the factors and associated metrics not only to track sources of instability or conflict in states and regions but also to prioritize allocation of resources. This would require development of a transparent approach that weights alternative metrics for each factor, and even the factors themselves.

Acknowledgments

The authors wish to thank a number of people who supported the study documented in this report. The study sponsor, Dr. William Crain, director, Center for Army Analysis (CAA), and E. B. Vandiver, former director, CAA, were extremely generous with their time in sharing insights on environments associated with IW and providing direction to the project. COL Steven Stoddard, division chief, Operations Analysis, was our point of contact and also offered valuable insights and guidance in several discussions; David Reynolds, deputy division chief, also provided valuable support. We wish to express our appreciation to Lauri Rohn, former director of RAND Arroyo Center's Strategy, Doctrine, and Resources Program, for her involvement in, encouragement of, and comments on our work and for the guidance she provided throughout the study. We also thank the current program director, Terry Kelly, and associate director, Karl Mueller, for their insights and for helping us bring the study to a conclusion.

We are indebted to Dr. John Arquilla, Professor and Chair, Department of Defense Analysis, Naval Postgraduate School; Ambassador John Herbst (Ret.), director of the Center for Complex Operations, National Defense University; Dr. Stathis Kalyvas, director, Program on Order, Conflict, and Violence, Yale University; Dr. Ziad Munson, associate professor of sociology, Lehigh University; Dr. Wilbur Scott, professor, Department of Behavioral Science and Leadership, U.S. Air Force Academy; COL G. L. Lamborn, U.S. Army Reserve (Ret.); and several other experts in IW, sociology, anthropology, and political science with whom we shared our results and who provided extensive comments on the factors we identified. We also presented our study and results to the U.S. Army's Senior Analysts Group at RAND in February 2012 and received very insightful and helpful feedback from the participants. Without the help of these experts, the authors would not have been able to complete the research.

We greatly appreciate the thoughtful and insightful comments provided by the three reviewers of the draft: Dr. Anna Simons, Naval Postgraduate School, and RAND colleagues Christopher Paul and Agnes Schaefer. Their extensive reviews of a draft significantly strengthened the substance and organization of the report.

Many thanks go to a number of RAND colleagues who provided insights during a roundtable and subsequent informal discussions: Paul Davis, Eric Larson, Arturo Muñoz, Frank Camm, Wade Markel, Colin Clarke, and Douglas Yeung. Tom Szayna offered useful advice during a number of discussions with the project leader and team. These colleagues made early, important contributions to the development of our factor matrix and analytic framework.

Finally, we appreciate the considerable support we received from Francisco Walter and Stephanie Lonsinger for helping prepare the manuscript. And many thanks to Nora Spiering for carefully editing the document.

Abbreviations

CAA	Center for Army Analysis
CALL	Center for Army Lessons Learned
COIN	counterinsurgency
CSSM	computer-supported social movement
DoD	U.S. Department of Defense
EZLN	Ejército Zapatista de Liberación Nacional [Zapatista National Liberation Army]
FARC	Fuerzas Armadas Revolucionarias de Colombia [Revolutionary Armed Forces of Colombia]
FATA	Federally Administered Tribal Areas
FM	field manual
IO	information operations
IW	irregular warfare
JOC	Joint Operating Concept
NGO	nongovernmental organization
PCC	Partido Comunista de Colombia [Communist Party of Colombia]
SOF	special operations forces
UNDP	United Nations Development Program

CHAPTER ONE

Introduction

Despite doctrinal treatment of conflicts categorized as "irregular warfare" (IW), defense analysts have found it challenging to identify what underlying factors matter in particular conflicts or unstable environments. As a result, they have had difficulty developing analytic games and models that explore these factors and identify means of ameliorating their contribution to conflict. The objective of this report is to help defense analysts identify and assess key factors that create and perpetuate environments in which destabilizing conditions arise—and become vulnerable to insurgency, terrorism, and other extremist violence—and to enable them to inform military decisions on allocating resources globally across areas of instability and within nations encountering instability. The report focuses in particular on sources of understanding about these environments from the fields of sociology, cultural anthropology, and political science and documents the development and vetting of 12 factors identified or substantiated in the research.

The 2012 strategic guidance of the U.S. Department of Defense (DoD) states that violent extremists will continue to threaten U.S. interests, allies, partners, and the homeland, and therefore affirms counterterrorism and IW as a primary mission of the U.S. armed forces.[1] Emphasizing that "global counterterrorism efforts will become more widely distributed" as U.S. forces depart from Afghanistan, the guidance asserts that the United States will counter violent extremists "by monitoring the activities of non-state threats world-wide, working with allies and partners to establish control over ungoverned territories, and directly striking the most dangerous groups and individuals when necessary."[2] Moreover, the U.S. armed forces will be prepared to conduct counterinsurgency (COIN) and stability operations that will feature "non-military means and military-to-military cooperation to address instability and reduce the demand for significant U.S. force commitments to stability operations."[3]

DoD defines IW as

> a violent struggle among state and non-state actors for legitimacy and influence over the relevant population(s). Irregular warfare favors indirect and asymmetric approaches, though it may employ the full range of military and other capacities, in order to erode an adversary's power, influence, and will. Also called IW.[4]

---

[1] DoD, *Sustaining U.S. Global Leadership: Priorities for 21st Century Defense*, Washington, D.C., January 2012.

[2] DoD, 2012, p. 1.

[3] DoD, 2012, p. 6.

[4] DoD, *Department of Defense Dictionary of Military and Associated Terms*, Joint Publication 1-02, Washington, D.C., November 8, 2010a (as amended through December 15, 2012), p. 151.

IW has become a shorthand term for efforts to counter terrorists, insurgents, and other violent nonstate actors and to shore up the local authority's ability to govern, provide for the population, and attain legitimacy in the eyes of its citizens. In this report, however, we use the term carefully in the context of DoD efforts and operations. More generally, we refer to environments that are vulnerable to conflict or insurgency and terrorism, as these environments may or may not be candidates for IW operations, particularly by the United States.

Conducting counterinsurgency, counterterrorism, stability, and other IW operations has placed large demands on U.S. ground forces. The current thinking reflected in the new guidance holds that these ground forces should emphasize non-kinetic operations—intended to persuade the population in areas affected or threatened by violent extremist groups to cooperate with the United States and its local partners and resist the activities of those groups. Engagement with partners to prevent conflict before it occurs ("Phase 0" operations) also minimizes both cost and the need for intervention with U.S. ground forces. Other DoD operational documents define an approach that "requires balance between defeating the threats and enhancing a local partner's legitimacy and influence over a population by addressing the causes of conflict and building the partner's ability to provide security, good governance and economic development."[5] However, military doctrine does not acknowledge that uncertainty exists among social scientists about the salience of some of these causes in general, as well as in specific conflicts. Appendix A briefly describes what doctrine has to say about causes of unstable environments that might require the United States and its partners to engage in IW.

By providing an understanding of how unstable, violence-prone environments are created and perpetuated, this report can help analysts decide which states or regions appear most susceptible to instability and which may require in-depth analysis, gaming, and modeling on what matters in those environments. It draws key factors from the fields of sociology, anthropology, and political science that play a role in creating, perpetuating, and mitigating destabilizing conditions that facilitate growth of violent extremist organizations. Sociology and anthropology in particular have been accorded less in-depth review by defense analysts than political, economic, and other fields, though key surveys and accompanying analyses at the RAND Corporation and elsewhere have been conducted across multiple social science disciplines.[6] This report examines existing sociological, anthropological, and related schools of thought, theories, and models that could advance understanding of the cultural and social factors that give rise to environments in which DoD application of its IW capabilities may become necessary and improve analysis of the factors that might encourage people to support violent actors. This is not a comprehensive review or even a survey of all social science research on war, small wars, or instability. Rather, it is a selective review of anthropological and sociological work—as well as related political science research—relevant to the sponsor's interests and fitting into an agreed-upon factor-driven approach. Moreover, the report does not purport to identify when or where DoD IW efforts should be engaged; as such, terms other than IW are used to describe the environments and actors under consideration.

---

[5]   DoD, *Irregular Warfare: Countering Irregular Threats*, Joint Operating Concept, Version 2.0, May 2010b, p. 7.

[6]   Paul K. Davis and Kim Cragin, eds., *Social Science for Counterterrorism: Putting the Pieces Together*, Santa Monica, Calif.: RAND Corporation, MG-849-OSD, 2009.

Sociology and Anthropology in DoD's Irregular Warfare Context

Social science has been used as a means for understanding the motivations of violent nonstate actors and populations that these actors (and the governments they are challenging) seek to influence. Sociologists and cultural anthropologists have approached the study of unstable environments prone to conflict in very different ways.

The terrorist attacks on the United States on September 11, 2001, provided the impetus for a proliferation of sociological research into these environments. Sociologists sought to apply their theories and schools of thought to understand the underlying causes of terrorism and insurgency and to offer means of addressing some of these causes. They have utilized a wide range of constructs, including conflict theory, social movement theory, social network theory, and institutional or organizational theory.

Anthropological inquiries tend to use long-term ethnographic studies of particular groups as their primary evidence base. In contrast with sociology, the field of cultural anthropology has produced fewer studies on the foundations of environments that could give rise to DoD involvement in IW. Since World War II, and even after 9/11, the field generally has repudiated assistance to the military or other official state actors, and actively censures such work. One reason for this is the belief among many anthropologists that they should not conduct research that could influence the very populations that serve as the objects of their work. Another reason for this smaller set of anthropological studies is that anthropologists do not commonly conduct ethnographies during active conflict. However, a smaller group of anthropologists has done excellent ethnographic work through research on insurgent groups and dynamics in and around war zones, and some have broken the mold and worked directly with DoD on IW and counterinsurgency campaigns and operations.

Research Approach and Road Map to This Report

The U.S. Army asked RAND to shed light on social science approaches to understanding environments in which violent extremist groups exist. The RAND team pursued three tasks. First, the team surveyed existing sociological, anthropological, political science, and other social science theories and schools of thought as to the main sources of instability that could nurture violent extremist groups. We reviewed a broad range of literature in these fields, including journal articles, books, and recent RAND work and that of other research centers. This included some ethnographies, although an exhaustive review of extensive anthropological treatment of numerous groups was not within the scope of the study. The review also included relevant literature in other fields (such as political science) to shed light on potential interactions with sociological and anthropological theories. Chapter Two provides an overview of the literature review and describes some of the major theoretical underpinnings of sociological, anthropological, and other approaches to conflict-prone environments.

From this literature review, the RAND team drew out and framed key factors that appear to create and perpetuate these environments and then discerned areas of consensus among social scientists regarding the salience of these factors. We vetted the 12 factors by comparing them with those in recent RAND research on 30 insurgencies[7] and then reviewed them with over a dozen social scientists both inside and outside RAND. The RAND team also identified a number of important characteristics of each factor, including mitigating and exacerbating circumstances, examples of conflicts in which the factor was present, and descriptive models or narratives associated with the factor in the literature. Chapter Three describes each factor and its attendant characteristics and assesses the level of expert consensus about its salience. Chapter Four posits the interrelationships among the factors in two recent cases of COIN selected by the study sponsor.

It should be noted that cultural anthropology generally does not seek to establish consensus about variables or causal factors—either in general or with respect to the particular problem set at hand. As such, anthropological debates were used to identify lack of consensus but almost never to establish consensus (which was more often derived from the sociology and political science literature). Our factor-based approach is not easily reconciled with the ethnographic methods used by most cultural anthropologists, which tend to focus on the historical and local cultural specifics of each conflict. We have sought to incorporate ethnographically based observations into the factors as much as possible, but the minutiae and subtleties revealed by ethnography often do not fit well into a general factor-based approach. However, the factor-based approach is more accessible to defense analysts seeking to quickly identify regional "hot spots" for more in-depth focus and can help them narrow in on specific ethnographies to improve understanding of such hot spots in greater detail.

In a third task, the RAND team identified qualitative and quantitative metrics that could be used in analysis of environments in which the factors may play a role. These metrics were drawn from the literature review, suggestions emerging from expert interviews, and previous RAND research. Chapter Five explores candidate metrics and potential data sources for each of the factors and posits ways in which the metrics might be used analytically. Chapter Six offers findings, recommendations, and concluding remarks. Following Appendix A on doctrine (mentioned above), Appendix B contains a matrix (which is described in Chapter Three) that summarizes the factors and their main characteristics. Appendix C presents a cross-matching of factors introduced in this study with ones identified in the aforementioned RAND research on 30 insurgencies.[8]

---

[7] Christopher Paul, Colin P. Clarke, and Beth Grill, *Victory Has a Thousand Fathers: Detailed Counterinsurgency Case Studies,* Santa Monica, Calif.: RAND Corporation, MG-964/1-OSD, 2010.

[8] Paul, Clarke, and Grill, 2010.

CHAPTER TWO

Gaining Insights into Unstable, Conflict-Prone Environments Through Social Science Lenses

Introduction

The social sciences provide a theoretical base to explain how and in what ways unstable, violent environments emerge and propagate. The purpose of this chapter is to briefly describe the major theories that sociology, anthropology, and other fields use to study unstable environments, including what causes conflict, insurgency, or terrorism by violent nonstate actors. We start with brief descriptions of relevant sociological theories and then address anthropological theories based on a literature review of relevant publications. We also briefly touch on key theories and concepts explored in political science and microeconomics that contribute to our understanding of these environments. We conclude the chapter with a summary of the key points from our review of the literature. This literature review and inventory of key theories forms the foundation for the factors that we describe in Chapter Three.

Sociological Theories

Sociology has long examined how societies are stratified along a variety of lines (for example, racial/ethnic, gender, class, political power, status, religion, or national origin), how this stratification causes conflict, what motivates people to collective action in riots or revolutions, and the causes of crime and deviance or social ostracism. Nevertheless, since 2001, sociological frameworks and theories have been increasingly applied to the study of unstable, conflict-prone environments of interest to analysts dealing with IW. This section summarizes the primary theoretical traditions that we determined to be the most relevant for understanding insurgency, terrorism, and the rise and sustainment of violent nonstate actors: conflict theory, social movement theory, social network theory, and institutional (organizational) theory.

Conflict Theory

Conflict theory argues that the unequal distribution of power and resources within societies produces conflicts. These conflicts have the power to transform existing social relations in that society.[1] Following this line of thought, the interests of the elites in a society are in direct opposition to those who are not in positions of power or authority. The politically or economically

---

[1] Randall Collins, *Four Sociological Traditions: Selected Readings*, Oxford, UK: Oxford University Press, 1994; and C. Wright Mills, *Power, Politics, and People: The Collected Essays of C. Wright Mills,* Oxford, UK: Oxford University Press, 1963.

disadvantaged therefore have interests that run counter to the status quo. These conflicting interests foment social change.[2] This theory is widely applied to historical case studies of civil war or revolution in which a state governed by a ruling elite was overthrown by a local population that was either politically marginalized or economically distressed.

Sociological studies often point to the influence of relative deprivation and the perception of group marginalization[3] in the emergence of civil wars or revolutions. Relative deprivation refers to the negative perception that differences exist between wants and actualities, with perceived inequalities being as powerful as actual ones. This is because when members of a society become dissatisfied or frustrated with their social, economic, and political situation, they yearn for changes. Social scientists have long noted that the actual conditions that people live under may not be at fault, but people's perceptions of their conditions are.[4]

Social Movement Theory

Social movement theory offers a conceptual framework for understanding how and why collective action and political contention (violence, terrorism, or insurgency) emerge. Social movement theory posits that individuals are moved to collective action in three ways: through the mobilization of resources, the provision of opportunities afforded within a wider political context, and the framing of the messages and rhetoric of the organizers of a movement.[5]

Resource mobilization theory argues that for movements or insurgent efforts to emerge and sustain themselves, a foundation and the constant flow of material, financial, and human resources need to exist.[6] The success of a movement therefore depends on the extent to which it can marshal these resources. Beck argues that modern-day violent nonstate actors are organized much like social movement organizations: a highly professionalized core that directs and manages attacks, assembles resources, and provides overall leadership to a broader base of supporters.[7] Resource mobilization theory is therefore applicable to long-standing terrorist groups, such as Hamas, the Tamil Tigers, and Hezbollah, which organize themselves into quasigovernments in the territories they control while still undertaking militant actions.[8]

---

[2]   Alan Sears, *A Good Book, In Theory: A Guide to Theoretical Thinking,* North York, Toronto: Higher Education University of Toronto Press, 2008.

[3]   Relative inequality and group marginalization refer, respectively, to one group having more access to resources than another and to one group having particularly low access to resources vis-à-vis other groups.

[4]   Ted Gurr, *Why Men Rebel,* Princeton, N.J.: Princeton University Press, 1970.

[5]   Colin Beck, "The Contribution of Social Movement Theory to Understanding Terrorism," *Sociology Compass,* Vol. 2, No. 5, 2008, pp. 1565–1581; Doug McAdam, John D. McCarthy, and Mayer N. Zald, "Introduction: Opportunities, Mobilizing Structures, and Framing Processes—Toward a Synthetic, Comparative Perspective on Social Movements," in Doug McAdam, John D. McCarthy, and Mayer N. Zald, eds., *Comparative Perspectives on Social Movements: Political Opportunities, Mobilizing Structures, and Cultural Framings,* Cambridge, UK: Cambridge University Press, 1996, pp. 1–20; Doug McAdam, Sidney Tarrow, and Charles Tilly, "To Map Contentious Politics," *Mobilization,* Vol. 1, 1996, pp. 17–34; Doug McAdam, Sidney Tarrow, and Charles Tilly, *Dynamics of Contention,* Cambridge, UK: Cambridge University Press, 2001; and Sidney Tarrow, *Power in Movement: Social Movements and Contentious Politics,* Cambridge, UK: Cambridge University Press, 1998.

[6]   John D. McCarthy and Mayer N. Zald, "Resource Mobilization and Social Movements: A Partial Theory," *American Journal of Sociology,* Vol. 82, No. 6, 1977, pp. 1212–1241.

[7]   Beck, 2008.

[8]   J. Craig Jenkins, "Resource Mobilization Theory and the Study of Social Movements," *Annual Review of Sociology,* Vol. 9, 1983, pp. 527–553.

Political process theory posits that overall political and social conditions must be ripe for successful and sustained violence or contention.[9] The opportunity for mobilization may result from large shifts in the overall political structure, or events may provide specific opportunities for an instance of contentious action. Even the perception of an opportunity may motivate collective action, as Kurzman argues in the case of the Iranian Revolution.[10] Recent research on Islamic mobilization in the Middle East has also used a political opportunities approach, seeing an opportunity for Islamic movements in the opening of participatory politics in some countries.[11] Beck uses al Qaeda in Iraq as an example of an insurgent group that arises not just from grievances or the mobilization of resources but also because of the political opportunity: The American invasion demolished centralized authority, creating the opportunity for new mobilization and a threat to established power arrangements.

Framing theory examines how successful opposition forces or groups make claims that resonate with wider social narratives to gain popularity,[12] a process called *frame alignment*.[13] The meaning that participants ascribe to their actions is a central part of mobilization.[14] Framing has been found to be an important aspect of many instances of collective action, including such issue-driven movements as antiglobalization,[15] mass riots,[16] and Islamic militancy.[17] Like other movements, insurgent groups spend much time and effort in justifying and explaining their efforts. For example, ideological manifestos, calls to action, speeches, and communiqués to supporters and potential supporters are routine aspects of insurgent campaigns.[18]

The three-pronged framework of social movement theory came into widespread use in the 1990s as a response to the dominant theories at the time, predicated on conflict theory, that

---

[9]   Doug McAdam, *Political Process and the Development of Black Insurgency, 1930–1970*, Chicago, Ill.: University of Chicago Press, 1982.

[10]   Charles Kurzman, "Structural Opportunity and Perceived Opportunity in Social-Movement Theory: The Iranian Revolution of 1979," *American Sociological Review*, Vol. 61, No. 1, pp. 153–170; and Charles Kurzman, *The Unthinkable Revolution in Iran,* Cambridge, Mass.: Harvard University Press, 2004.

[11]   Mohammed M. Hafez, *Why Muslims Rebel: Repression and Resistance in the Islamic World*, Boulder, Colo.: Lynne Rienner Publishers, 2003; and Jillian Schwedler, *Faith in Moderation: Islamist Parties in Jordan and Yemen*, New York: Cambridge University Press, 2006.

[12]   William A. Gamson, *The Strategy of Social Protest*, Homewood, Ill.: Dorsey Press, 1975; and William A. Gamson, *Talking Politics*, New York: Cambridge University Press, 1992.

[13]   David A. Snow, E. Burke Rochford, Jr., Steven K. Worden, and Robert D. Benford, "Frame Alignment Processes, Micromobilization, and Movement Participation," *American Sociological Review*, Vol. 51, No. 4, 1986, pp. 464–481; and Robert D. Benford and David A. Snow, "Framing Processes and Social Movements: An Overview and Assessment," *Annual Review of Sociology*, Vol. 26, 2000, pp. 611–639.

[14]   Doug McAdam, "Tactical Innovation and the Pace of Insurgency," *American Sociological Review*, Vol. 48, No. 6, 1983, pp. 735–754; Francesca Polletta, "'It Was Like a Fever…': Narrative and Identity in Social Protest," *Society for the Study of Social Problems*, Vol. 45, No. 2, 1998, pp. 137–159; and Francesca Polletta, *It Was Like a Fever: Storytelling in Protest and Politics,* Chicago, Ill.: University of Chicago Press, 2006.

[15]   Jeffrey M. Ayres, "Framing Collective Action Against Neoliberalism: The Case of the Anti-Globalization Movement," *Journal of World-Systems Research*, Vol. 10, No. 1, 2004, pp. 10–34.

[16]   David A. Snow, Rens Vliegenthart, and Catherine Corrigall-Brown, "Framing the French Riots: A Comparative Study of Frame Variation," *Social Forces*, Vol. 86, No. 2, 2007, pp. 385–415.

[17]   David A. Snow and Scott C. Byrd, "Ideology, Framing Processes, and Islamic Terrorist Movements," *Mobilization*, Vol. 12, No. 1, pp. 119–136.

[18]   Beck, 2008.

collective action and social movements were primarily caused by political or economic griev-ances, perceptions of relative economic deprivation or political repression, or social strain.[19] For example, Gurr[20] views the relative deprivation of a group as a central factor in the emergence of contention, and Kornhauser[21] argues that alienation from mass society motivates individuals to participate in collective action. These classic models focused on understanding what motivated individuals to challenge the status quo,[22] investigating individuals' perceived opportunity costs and incentives to engage in risky collective action.[23]

In the study of unstable environments susceptible to political violence, grievance and strain theories certainly have merit. Many studies have found that insurgents or violent non-state actors are motivated by threatened values or idealized religious doctrine in contradiction with society's practice,[24] reactions to the strain of modernization in society,[25] foreign military occupations and external influence,[26] or other broad grievances.[27] However, social movement theory recognizes that grievances, relative deprivation or repression, or social strains alone are not enough to explain why some motivations become organized into sustained contention and movements and others do not.[28]

Social Network Theory

Social network theory is another sociological area of inquiry that holds promise for under-standing the emergence and sustainability of collective action, and therefore of insurgency.[29] Social network theory provides a framework to examine the structure of networks[30] and the strength of ties among members of a network[31]—and therefore the possibility of points where connections could be broken as part of counterinsurgent efforts.[32]

---

[19] Neil J. Smelser, *Theory of Collective Behavior,* Glencoe, Ill.: Free Press of Glencoe, 1963; and Gary T. Marx and James L. Wood, "Strands of Theory and Research in Collective Behavior," *Annual Review of Sociology*, Vol. 1, 1975, pp. 363–428.

[20] Gurr, 1970.

[21] William Kornhauser, *The Politics of Mass Society,* Glencoe, Ill.: The Free Press of Glencoe, 1959.

[22] McAdam, 1982.

[23] Mancur Olson, *The Logic of Collective Action: Public Goods and the Theory of Groups*, Cambridge, Mass.: Harvard University Press, 1965.

[24] Mark Juergensmeyer, *Terror in the Mind of God: The Global Rise of Religious Violence*, Berkeley, Calif.: University of California Press, 2003.

[25] Mervyn F. Bendle, "Militant Religion and the Crisis of Modernity: A New Paradigm," *Research in the Social Scientific Study of Religion,* Vol. 14, 2003, pp. 229–252.

[26] Mohammed Ayoob, "The Future of Political Islam: The Importance of External Variables," *International Affairs*, Vol. 81, No. 5, 2005, pp. 951–961; and Robert Pape, *Dying to Win: The Strategic Logic of Suicide Terrorism*, New York: Random House, 2005.

[27] Jessica Stern, *Terror in the Name of God: Why Religious Militants Kill*, New York: Ecco, 2003.

[28] John D. McCarthy and Mayer N. Zald, "The Trend of Social Movements in America: Professionalization and Resource Mobilization," Morristown, N.J.: General Learning Press, 1973; and McCarthy and Zald, 1977.

[29] Marc Sageman, *Understanding Terror Networks*, Philadelphia, Pa.: University of Pennsylvania Press, 2004.

[30] Ami Pedahzur and Arie Perliger, "The Changing Nature of Suicide Attacks: A Social Network Perspective," *Social Forces*, Vol. 84, No. 4, 2006, pp. 1987–2008.

[31] Mark Granovetter, "The Strength of Weak Ties," *The American Journal of Sociology*, Vol. 78, No. 6, 1973, pp. 1360–1380.

[32] Jonathan David Farley, "Breaking al Qaeda Cells: A Mathematical Analysis of Counterterrorism Operations (A Guide for Risk Assessment and Decision Making)," *Studies in Conflict & Terrorism*, Vol. 26, 2003, pp. 399–411; and Kathleen M.

Social network theories argue that the structure of a network and the number and types of relationships among group members can be a determinant in an individual's success and decisionmaking processes, the identity of the most influential individuals, the likely behavior of the group, and the group's responses to internal and external shocks. In social network theory, the attributes of individuals are less important than their ties and relationships with other actors within the network. Social network theories explore and measure relationships and interactions among individual actors in the network, also known as nodes, and use network diagrams to understand the flow of power, resources (money, facilities, or equipment), and information through the organization and how network connections affect the recruitment of supporters.[33] McAdam and Paulsen find that individuals are more likely to join a movement if their friends, family, and other acquaintances are already participants.[34] Gould argues that network ties among participants increase solidarity and the intensity of contention.[35] Because actors and their actions are viewed as interdependent rather than as independent, autonomous units, the linkages between and among actors are channels for transfer or "flow" of resources (either material or nonmaterial). The environment of the network therefore provides opportunities for, or constraints on, individual actions.[36]

In the study of crime and deviance, sociologists have argued that social relationships and how connected one is to others can have a role in determining an individual's or a group's propensity for violence. This is called social bond theory,[37] and recently it has been used as a possible explanatory factor for insurgency.[38] Griffith explains that "weak social bonds lead to higher levels of delinquency or violence in a population."[39] Social bonds can be grouped into four categories:

1. **attachments**: an individual's attachments to others (weak attachments lead to insensitivity to opinions of others)
2. **commitments**: an individual's investment in conventional behavior (stronger investments lead to greater perception of risks in delinquent behavior)
3. **beliefs**: an individual's support for conventional norms (lack of perception of validity of social rules of behavior)
4. **involvements**: amount of time spent on conventional activities like school or employment (lack of involvements provides more free time to engage in delinquent behavior).

Carley, "Destabilization of Covert Networks," *Computational & Mathematical Organization Theory*, Vol. 12, No. 1, 2006, pp. 51–66.

[33] McAdam, 1983.

[34] Doug McAdam and Ronnelle Paulsen, "Specifying the Relationship Between Social Ties and Activism," *American Journal of Sociology*, Vol. 99, No. 3, 1993, pp. 640–667.

[35] Roger V. Gould, "Multiple Networks and Mobilization in the Paris Commune, 1871," *American Sociological Review*, Vol. 56, No. 6, 1991, pp. 716–729.

[36] Stanley Wasserman and Katherine Faust, *Social Network Analysis: Methods and Applications (Structural Analysis in the Social Sciences)*, Cambridge, UK: Cambridge University Press, 1994.

[37] Travis Hirschi, *Causes of Delinquency*, New Brunswick, N.J.: Transaction Publishers, 2002; and James Q. Wilson and Joan Petersilia, eds., *Crime*, San Francisco, Calif.: Institute for Contemporary Studies, 1995.

[38] Kevin Griffith, "The People Are the Prize: Socials Bonds as a Counterinsurgency Objective," *Phalanx*, December 2010, pp. 10–13.

[39] Griffith, 2010, p. 10.

Social media is one method by which individuals or groups in social networks can connect. It will be discussed more thoroughly in Chapter Three.

Institutional/Organizational Theory

Another set of sociological theories examines how the institutional environments and social structures within which individuals are situated (e.g., schools, places of work, families, and even political or economic structures) and the ways in which those institutions and structures can create norms, beliefs, or routines that organize individuals and guide their social behavior and decisions become established, adopted, and then even adapted over time and across regions or social groups.[40] When considered in the context of insurgency, this theory can help examine how insurgent groups create and use norms of social behavior to manipulate local populations to join the group. However, to date, this theory is not as well studied in this context as the previous theories.

Anthropological Theories

Much anthropological work has focused on understanding the drivers of warfare in preindustrial populations.[41] In some cases, such analyses have taken a deep historical or even evolutionary view, applying the analysis of resource scarcity and reproductive competition[42] within and among societies to yield insights into the dynamics and drivers of warfare over time.[43] This bird's-eye view of the fundamental drivers of conflict is strongly rooted in the anthropological subdisciplines of evolutionary anthropology, biological anthropology, and archeology. Meanwhile, cultural and psychological anthropology have taken a more fine-grained approach to examining how child-rearing practices, cultural values and beliefs, and even media content can work to produce and maintain conflict, violence, and war within societies.

Many of anthropology's insights regarding the drivers of conflict are derived from detailed, locally grounded observations and historical analysis. This analytic process often involves long periods of time spent collecting data *in situ* to establish intimate familiarity with a cultural context. The detailed historical and cultural analysis that results from such ethnographic work also favors a narrative format over numbers or variables. As such, ethnographically based anthropology lends itself less to the development and testing of discrete factors leading to instability or other dynamics involved in unstable environments—and more to rich and detailed case studies. This report uses factors and variables to describe drivers of instability and conflict—an approach more typical of sociology or political science than anthropology.

Of course, ethnographic case studies can be used to validate or question the importance of individual factors. But perhaps the greatest strength of an ethnographic approach is that it illustrates the complex, historically contingent process by which factors and processes come together in unique ways within different conflicts to drive conflict and instability. This

---

[40] Walter W. Powell and Paul J. DiMaggio, eds., *The New Institutionalism in Organizational Analysis*, Chicago, Ill.: University of Chicago Press, 1991.

[41] J. Haas, ed., *The Anthropology of War*, Cambridge, UK: Cambridge University Press, 1990.

[42] In other words, competitive access to food and sexual partners.

[43] N. A. Chagnon, "Life Histories, Blood Revenge, and Warfare in a Tribal Population," *Science*, Vol. 239, No. 4843, 1988, pp. 985–992.

dynamic, locally grounded approach is best captured in the format of ethnography itself and is specific to particular time periods and geographic regions. While this report takes a factor- or variable-based approach to the drivers of instability and conflict, the approach reserves a role for ethnographies to provide "deep dives" on individual instances of conflict. Due to limitations of scope, space, and resources, this approach is not fully explicated in this report. However, we direct the reader to the references cited in this section or recent anthropological anthologies on war and violence as starting points for further reading.[44]

The following section describes key areas of theory and research across anthropological subdisciplines regarding how such factors and dynamics can produce environments prone to insurgency and terrorism. It is important to note that these theoretical areas were extracted selectively in support of our factor-driven approach to instability. They do not, as such, represent consensus within the field of anthropology as drivers of instability or IW.

Cultures of Violence

Anthropologists have directed considerable attention to explaining how some groups come to display markedly higher levels of violence than other groups. In doing so, they have focused on exploring the cultural origins of violence—specifically, the rituals and traditions within groups that infuse individuals with the propensity or tendency to attack and harm others, along with the narratives and themes that societies use to justify or even glorify violent acts.

One anthropological test case is Papua New Guinea, where anthropologists have documented how the ritual transition to manhood among boys involves traumatic experiences and aggressive themes that help prepare young boys for conflict and war—mainly through triggering negative emotions and framing aggression as critical for the proper assumption of male roles.[45] In the same vein, Bourgois describes how physical violence in poor urban environments is rooted in traumatic childhood experiences and is exacerbated by cultural themes and rituals that glorify violent masculinity.[46] In particular, Bourgois emphasizes the role of poverty and inequality in perpetuating the social conditions that produce and maintain cultures of violence.

Anthropological approaches to cultures of violence often take an explicitly comparative approach; for example, Fry shows how two communities a short distance from each other can show dramatically different patterns of adult aggression and how these community differences in aggression are created by differences in child-rearing practices and patterns of social interaction.[47] More directly related to conflict environments, Allen describes how Palestinian culture

---

[44] N. Scheper-Hughes and P. Bourgois, *Violence in War and Peace: An Anthology*, Malden, Mass.: Blackwell Publishing, 2003.

[45] D. F. Tuzin, "Ritual Violence Among Ilahita Arapesh: The Dynamics of Moral and Religious Uncertainty," in G. H. Herdt., ed., *Rituals of Manhood: Male Initiation in Papua New Guinea*, Berkeley, Calif.: University of California Press, 1982, pp. 321–355; and G. Herdt, "Aspects of Socialization for Aggression in Sambia Ritual and Warfare," *Anthropological Quarterly*, Vol. 59, No. 4, 1986, pp. 160–164.

[46] P. Bourgois, "In Search of Masculinity: Violence, Respect and Sexuality Among Puerto Rican Crack Dealers in East Harlem," *British Journal of Criminology*, Vol. 36, No. 3, 1996, pp. 412–427.

[47] D. P. Fry, "'Respect for the Rights of Others Is Peace': Learning Aggression Versus Nonaggression Among the Zapotec," *American Anthropologist*, Vol. 94, No. 3, 1992, pp. 621–639.

during the Second Intifada normalized the experience and practice of violence through the use of martyrdom themes.[48]

Cultures of Independence and Resistance

Instability is a core component of these environments, and this instability is often either enabled or directly caused by groups that resist the rule of centralized governance. In Scott's opinion, this resistance either can form among the lower socioeconomic rungs within a society,[49] or it can be endemic to certain social groups that have simply become accustomed to sustaining and ruling themselves in small groups without a central authority.[50] Such groups often display patterns of decentralized decisionmaking and dispute resolution in which legitimacy and enforcement occur at the localized, small-group level. Critical to such groups' resistance of central governance is a way to make a living that is difficult for the central government to track, control, or tax—such as herding animals; hunting and gathering; "slash and burn" agriculture; or even the production and trafficking of illegal substances, weapons, or people. Also critical is a sense of pride in a local identity that is superior to and/or not represented by the central government. While Scott focuses on the highlands of Southeast Asia to make his argument, Barfield has made similar arguments about Afghanistan,[51] and Kilcullen has done so about the Federally Administered Tribal Areas (FATA) in Pakistan.[52]

Inequality and Aggression

A third strain of anthropological thought relevant to the development of environments in which insurgency and terrorism can arise and perpetuate concerns the distribution of social status and resources in a population, instability or change in this distribution, and the production of violence. These insights come from both experimental and observational evidence over the last few decades collected on both human and nonhuman primates. Underlying this line of thought is the consistent observation that humans are naturally predisposed to seek social status to increase their access to resources and chances for reproduction. Environments with more unequal distribution of resources (i.e., a large and persistent underclass and a greater concentration of wealth among the few) have higher levels of physical violence,[53] as young males without resources perceive themselves to have limited life chances and engage in more desperate or dangerous acts in pursuit of social status, resources, and reproductive opportunities.[54]

---

[48] L. Allen, "Getting by the Occupation: How Violence Became Normal During the Second Palestinian Intifada," *Cultural Anthropology*, Vol. 23, No. 3, 2008, pp. 453–487.

[49] J. C. Scott, *Weapons of the Weak: Everyday Forms of Peasant Resistance,* New Haven, Conn.: Yale University Press, 1987.

[50] J. C. Scott, *The Art of Not Being Governed: An Anarchist History of Upland Southeast Asia*, New Haven, Conn.: Yale University Press, 2009.

[51] T. Barfield, "Culture and Custom in Nation-Building: Law in Afghanistan," *Maine Law Review*, Vol. 60, No. 2, 2008; Barnett R. Rubin, "Crafting a Constitution for Afghanistan," *Journal of Democracy*, Vol. 15, No. 3, 2004, pp. 5–19; and Olivier Roy, "Afghanistan: Back to Tribalism or on to Lebanon?" *Third World Quarterly*, Vol. 11, No. 4, 1989, pp. 70–82.

[52] David Kilcullen, *The Accidental Guerilla: Fighting Small Wars in the Midst of a Big One*, New York: Oxford University Press, 2009.

[53] R. G. Wilkinson, I. Kawachi, and B. P. Kennedy, "Mortality, the Social Environment, Crime and Violence," *Sociology of Health & Illness*, Vol. 20, No. 5, 1998, pp. 578–597.

[54] M. Daly, M. Wilson, and S. Vasdev, "Income Inequality and Homicide Rates in Canada and the United States," *Canadian Journal of Criminology*, Vol. 43, No. 2, 2001, pp. 219–236.

Of particular note is the observation that *instability* in the social hierarchy can lead to higher levels of stress and aggression within a population.[55] Thus, this anthropological line of thought is related not only to the role of poverty and socioeconomic inequality in producing insurgencies but also to the role of power vacuums caused by recent conflict or ungoverned space and the potential danger presented by groups that have recently gained or lost social status.

As Simons points out, the perception of being disenfranchised, even if it is not apparent from an outsider's perspective, can be a frequent motivator for mobilizing to conflict.[56] Similarly, Simons indicates that many insurgencies are founded on narratives of political exclusion.[57] Blending these understandings with framing theory (which was described in the "Sociological Theories" section) can help the analyst understand how groups and movements capitalize on and construct perceptions of inequality to mobilize individuals to violent action.

Local Systems of Social Control, Kinship Ties, and Identity

Many areas of emerging instability have vast areas into which state control has not reached (or from which it has recently receded). However, such areas are not without social rules to create order of some sort. As Simons points out, nonstate systems of regulating human behavior and enforcing order (including punishment for infractions) draw heavily on kinship.[58] In lieu of state systems that guarantee rights to individuals, systems based on familial or blood bonds and small-group membership will come to dominate, as these entities are able to provide protection from competing social groups, as well as resource-sharing and other functions. In this way, identity becomes a flexible and convenient form of social identification that can serve to facilitate survival, reproduction, and social or material gain. As such, understanding conflict also involves understanding the processes and mechanisms by which individuals adopt and express group identification.[59]

Anthropologists have pointed out how failing to understand local conceptions of identity and group affiliation—as well as local social systems for social regulation and conflict resolution—can lead to missed opportunities or mistakes in strategic planning, as well as operational and tactical errors (or, at the least, missed opportunities). For example, Katz describes how Afghan systems of social organization have traditionally been opposed to state rule and therefore most likely need to interact with state authorities through some sort of buffer organization.[60] Similarly, Keiser's detailed work on Kohistani conflict resolution highlights a system of revenge and blood feuds[61] that also works against the institution of Western notions of justice and related state-building efforts in Afghanistan (among the Pashtun).

---

[55] R. M. Sapolsky, "The Influence of Social Hierarchy on Primate Health," *Science*, Vol. 308, No. 5722, 2005, pp. 648–652.

[56] Anna Simons and David Tucker, "The Misleading Problem of Failed States: A 'Socio-Geography' of Terrorism in the Post-9/11 Era," *Third World Quarterly*, Vol. 28, No. 2, 2007, pp. 387–401.

[57] Anna Simons, "War: Back to the Future," *Annual Review of Anthropology*, Vol. 28, 1999, pp. 73–108.

[58] Anna Simons, "Democratisation and Ethnic Conflict: The Kin Connection," *Nations and Nationalism*, Vol. 3, No. 2, 1997, pp. 273–289.

[59] G. Schlee, *How Enemies Are Made: Towards a Theory of Ethnic and Religious Conflicts*, Berghahn Books, 2008.

[60] David Katz, "Reforming the Village War," *Middle East Quarterly*, Spring 2011, pp. 17–31.

[61] Lincoln Keiser, *Friend by Day, Enemy by Night: Organized Vengeance in a Kohistani Community*, Fort Worth, Tex.: Holt, Rinehart, and Winston, 1991.

In sum, understanding the complex, fluid, and overlapping forms of group identification is necessary for fully understanding the drivers of intergroup conflict. Furthermore, failing to account for local systems of justice, resource allocation, hierarchy, and other forms of social regulation (especially in the absence of effective state presence) lends itself to strategic mistakes and operational errors, especially with respect to stability operations and state-building efforts.

Other Social Science Theories and Unstable Environments

Several theoretical contributions from political science and microeconomics converge and overlap with some of the sociological and anthropological theories described previously. Two theoretical constellations in particular, the *rational choice* and *greed and grievance* paradigms, complement and enrich insights derived from the sociology and anthropology literature.

Rational Choice Theory

Rational choice theory, one of the key theoretical paradigms in political science and microeconomics, states that individuals choose the best action according to stable preferences and the constraints and incentives that they face.[62] When an individual makes decisions in the shadow of imperfect information and misperception, the individual can be described as operating within a *bounded rationality*. Many studies have examined whether violent nonstate actors, and terrorists in particular, behave as rational choice precepts predict.[63] The rational choice literature suggests that these actors weigh costs and benefits and select what appears to them to be the best action at both the tactical and strategic levels. For example, Robert Pape's examination of a large sample of suicide terrorist attacks from 1980 to 2001 concluded that even apparently irrational suicide terrorism behavior adheres to a "strategic logic" calculated to induce target government concessions.[64]

Rational choice theory has important implications for the emergence and persistence of environments that sustain insurgency and terrorism. Armed group personnel and target populations, the theory argues, make decisions about joining and supporting an armed group based on personal and groupwide incentives and constraints.

Greed and Grievance Theories

Greed and political grievance theories are a subset of constructs within the rational choice paradigm. At the core of the greed and grievance debate is whether economic and profit-seeking incentives (greed) tend to be a stronger or weaker motivational force for an armed group than ideological and political grievance incentives (grievance). Some scholars argue that the typical armed group's motivation for fighting stems from both economic and profit-seeking incentives

---

[62]   Kristen Renwick Monroe, "Psychology and Rational Actor Theory," *Political Psychology*, Vol. 16, No. 1, pp. 1–21.

[63]   For a review of research on "subrational" IW-relevant behavior, see Boaz Ganor, *The Counter-Terrorism Puzzle*, New Brunswick, N.J.: Transaction Publishers, 2005, and A. W. Kruglanski and S. Fishman, "The Psychology of Terrorism: 'Syndrome' Versus 'Tool' Perspectives," *Terrorism and Political Violence*, Vol. 18, No. 2, 2006, pp. 193–215.

[64]   R. A. Pape and J. K. Feldman, *Cutting the Fuse: The Explosion of Global Suicide Terrorism and How to Stop It*, Chicago, Ill.: University of Chicago Press, 2010.

and the desire to avenge political grievances.[65] Collier and Hoeffler, however, argue that "greed considerably outperforms grievance" in predicting the risk of civil wars and related conflict.[66] Their research is supported by findings from Berdal and Malone suggesting that international efforts to end civil wars have been undercut, at times, by the failure to account for key stakeholders' economic agendas.[67]

Some studies suggest that economic incentives shape what types of violent groups develop and how they behave. Weinstein argues that insurgencies in resource-rich environments use violence more indiscriminately and recruit soldiers more opportunistically with short-term material payoffs, relative to insurgencies in resource-poor environments. Weinstein's research suggests that resource-rich insurgencies are more violent but easier to dislodge when the group's resources are depleted.[68] In some cases, armed groups that are initially motivated by political grievance become dependent on illegal economic activities and shift their warfighting strategy to accommodate this dependency.

Greed and grievance theories offer an important lens for examining the role of government repression, corruption, external support, and exploitable resources in precipitating and perpetuating unstable, conflict-prone environments. At the very least, they highlight the importance of identifying the economic and ideological incentives and constraints of armed groups and target populations.

Concluding Remarks

This chapter summarized key theories from the social science fields of sociology, anthropology, political science, and microeconomics that can inform our understanding of how and why violent actions and insurgencies emerge.

Within sociology, conflict theory provides a foundation for understanding how social, economic, and political inequalities (whether perceived or real) can lead to disgruntlement and the rise of individuals to enact social change. Social movement theory provides an understanding of how the mobilization of resources, the opportunities afforded by the political context, and the framing of messages and rhetoric can galvanize a local population to collective action against a dominant state power. Social network theory provides a powerful lens through which to understand the interconnections of people within a society, how networks can be leveraged to recruit supporters for collective action, and how groups and organizations can dominate over individuals' wills or perceptions and actions. Social bond theory informs our understanding of how weak social bonds between individuals and attachments, commitments, norms, and beliefs within a society can lead to acts of violence. Institutional theory provides an under-

---

[65] Karen Ballentine and Jake Sherman, eds., *The Political Economy of Armed Conflict: Beyond Greed and Grievance*, Boulder, Colo.: Lynne Rienner Publishers, 2003.

[66] Paul Collier and Anke Hoeffler, "On Economic Causes of Civil War," *Oxford Economic Papers*, Vol. 50, No. 4, 1998, pp. 563–573; and Paul Collier and Anke Hoeffler, "Greed and Grievance in Civil War," *The Centre for the Study of African Economies Working Paper Series*, Working Paper 160, July 1, 2002.

[67] Mats R. Berdal and David Malone, *Greed and Grievance: Economic Agendas in Civil Wars*, Boulder, Colo.: Lynne Rienner Publishers, 2000.

[68] Jeremy Weinstein, *Inside Rebellion: The Politics of Insurgent Violence*, Cambridge, UK: Cambridge University Press, 2006.

standing of how social, political, and economic structures and environments create norms and rituals that authoritatively guide the behavior of individuals, which could lead some to join or promote insurgent groups.

The field of anthropology provides an understanding of how cultures of violence or independence can set the stage for conflict. It also illustrates how inequality and disenfranchisement are important motivators and narratives for collective action against states. Furthermore, anthropological thinking has illustrated how familial and blood bonds can act as security strategies for individuals in lieu of individual rights secured by stable governments. In addition, a lack of ability to recognize this and local systems of social control can thwart efforts to establish stability. Finally, rational choice theory, which examines how individuals make decisions, and greed and grievance theories, which are fundamental theories in the fields of political science and microeconomics, augment the sociological and anthropological theories.

Central to all of these theories is the examination of what motivates people to collective action and violence. While each theory provides plausible rationales to explain the emergence of insurgent and terrorist groups, the important element is the interplay between individuals' personal inclinations, beliefs, and positions in a society and the political, economic, and organizational structures in which they are situated. In the next chapter, we draw from these social science theories to articulate key factors that could be used to characterize the emergence and sustainment of unstable, conflict-prone environments.

CHAPTER THREE

Factors Associated with Environments Vulnerable to Conflict

Introduction

The previous chapter described anthropological, sociological, and related insights into the processes by which violence and instability are created and maintained over time (sometimes leading to intervention through IW operations). To formalize these insights from the abstract to the concrete and to ground them in particular examples, we developed a set of 12 key factors to describe these insights and their connection to instability. Our synthesis of the literature produced the following factors:

- Factor 1: Level of **external support** for violent, nonstate groups
- Factor 2: Extent to which the **government is considered illegitimate or ineffective** by the population
- Factor 3: Presence of tribal or ethnic indigenous populations with **history of resisting state rule** and/or cultures that encourage or justify violent behavior
- Factor 4: Levels of **poverty and inequality** or presence of one or more groups that have recently lost status or power
- Factor 5: Extent to which **local governance is fragmented, weak, or vulnerable** to replacement or co-option by nonstate group institutions
- Factor 6: Existence of **ungoverned space**
- Factor 7: Presence of **multiple violent, nonstate groups competing for power**
- Factor 8: **Level of government restriction on political or ideological dissent**; extent to which individuals feel alienated from governing process
- Factor 9: **Level of consistency/agreement** between nonstate group's goals and philosophy and preferences/worldview/ideology of target populations
- Factor 10: Extent to which population and nonstate **groups perceive faltering government commitment** to counterinsurgency campaign
- Factor 11: **Capacity, resources, and expertise of violent, nonstate groups**
- Factor 12: Pervasiveness of **social networks** capable of being galvanized and mobilized to resistant action.

We describe and characterize these factors' defining features and attributes in a matrix that is available in Appendix B. The matrix includes seven categories: key aspects, brief description, mitigating or exacerbating variables, metrics and data sources that could produce evidence for the factor, analytic questions that one could ask to determine whether the factor is probable in the environment, level of consensus of about the salience of the factor among experts in the field, and conflict examples.

This chapter first describes our methodological approach to compiling and validating the list of 12 key factors and the matrix we developed to characterize those factors' key defining features. We then describe the attributes of these factors in more detail, using the matrix as our touchstone.

Methodology for Validating the List of Factors and Their Characteristics

We vetted this set of factors and the accompanying descriptive matrix in two ways.[1] First, we drew from a set of 30 detailed COIN case studies produced for the RAND monograph *Victory Has a Thousand Fathers: Detailed Counterinsurgency Case Studies*, by Christopher Paul, Colin P. Clarke, and Beth Grill.[2] These case studies coded 75 micro-level factors (e.g., "insurgents' demonstrated potency through attacks," "expropriable cash crops or mineral wealth in area of conflict") for each case study examined. We cross-matched these 75 factors against our 12 factors to determine overlap; the results of this cross-matching can be found in Appendix C. We also analyzed each case study narrative to note the presence or absence of each of our 12 factors in these 30 case studies. As these case studies were focused on the resolution of COIN conflicts rather than the underlying factors leading to instability, we consider this validation strategy to be conservative. This strategy likely undercounts the presence of our 12 factors, as some factors may have also been present prior to violence and conflict. Through this analytic process, we were able to determine that each of our 12 factors played a role in an average of nine out of 30 conflicts (minimum two, maximum 25).[3]

The second way in which we validated our list of factors was to consult eight RAND experts and eleven external experts on social movements, environments vulnerable to extremist violence, and insurgencies, including sociologists, anthropologists, and political scientists.[4] We compiled a list of potential experts outside of RAND from references consulted for the literature review and from suggestions by internal and external experts we interviewed.[5]

We conducted interviews between January and April 2012. Each interview lasted 60–90 minutes, during which RAND research team members took detailed notes and recorded the interview for fact-checking purposes. Before each interview, experts were given a brief description of the intent of the study, a draft of the list of factors that RAND research team members had synthesized from our review of the literature, and a matrix describing key characteristics of the factors. We asked interviewees to answer the following types of questions:

---

[1]   A third method to validate the factor list and accompanying matrix would have been to conduct a formal Delphi exercise to refine the model or better structure the expert validation process. We would recommend that future work on factors conduct a formal exercise such as the one described in Christopher Paul, Russell W. Glenn, Beth Grill, Megan McKernan, Barbara Raymond, Matthew Stafford, and Horacio R. Trujillo, "Identifying Urban Flashpoints: A Delphi-Derived Model for Scoring Cities' Vulnerability to Large Scale Unrest," *Studies in Conflict and Terrorism*, Vol. 31, No. 1, 2008, pp. 981–1000. We thank a reviewer for pointing this out.

[2]   Paul, Clarke, and Grill, 2010.

[3]   The exception was social networking technologies (a component of Factor 12), which were featured only once because most of the COIN examples were not recent cases.

[4]   RAND and federal human subjects policy forbids the identification of individuals without their consent. Most interviews were conducted on a nonattribution basis.

[5]   We recognize that this method of sample selection did not result in an exhaustive list of potential experts. However, this method produced a cohesive list of experts on a wide range of the topics.

- Have we adequately captured factors related to violence by nonstate actors recognized through research in the fields of anthropology, sociology, and related research?
- If not, are there better ways of framing the factors? Should any be combined? Are there additional factors we may have missed?
- What is your sense of the relative importance of each of the factors?
- Which ones seem to be generally salient across a wide range of cases, and which are highly dependent on specific cases and conditions?
- Which factors do you believe enjoy broad consensus among social scientists, and which are more contentious?
- Of the ones where there is broad consensus, are there any important studies that disagree but are considered "outliers"?
- What are examples of host-nation or supporting-nation actions that have alleviated or exacerbated the effect of these factors?
- What metrics might we use to measure the presence and/or effect of each factor?
- What data could be collected to enable such measurement? Are the data readily available?

Analysis of the information provided by the interviewed experts resulted in significant revision to the factor list. In some cases, experts also provided written feedback on the accompanying matrix. Experts also discussed a wide range of ancillary information for each factor, such as the degree of consensus in the field and application of factors to specific conflict examples.

Key Factors and Their Attributes

In this section we provide detailed descriptions of each factor, using the factor matrix in Appendix B as a guide and source of input, focusing on a portion of the information provided within the matrix:

- factor title
- overview
- key aspects
- mitigating variables
- conflict examples
- consensus in the literature.

Factor title is a reference we assign to the factor that is meant to be descriptive of the phenomenon across several social science studies. Our title may or may not match the names given in each of the studies themselves.

Overview elaborates on the "Brief Description" column in the matrix, providing more detail and explanation. This overview helps ensure recognition and understanding of a factor and helps to distinguish it from other factors, especially when there are similarities or overlapping terms associated with multiple factors.

Our treatment of *key aspects* provides further information on each factor, including theoretical basis and models, as well as case examples. This section also describes relationships with other factors (if applicable).

Mitigating variables refer to influences on the factor that affect its strength and importance in a given conflict or scenario. For example, a factor referring to historical resistance to central authority would be influenced by the presence of subcultures glorifying violence as a means of interaction by tribes with external actors. Likewise, the importance of communication and social media as a factor in creating or perpetuating unstable, violence-prone environments would be influenced by popular tolerance of radical political messages. Essentially, these mitigating or exacerbating variables are subfactors that affect the salience of factors in particular environments.

Conflict examples documents sample instances in which the literature has postulated that the factor has played a role in the development of an insurgency, terrorist group, or other violent organization. At times, these conflicts are themselves case studies found in the scholarly literature; in other instances, the conflicts are mentioned as examples where a factor is manifested.

Level of consensus describes the level of importance ascribed to a factor in creating or sustaining violence in a region by social scientists. We determined the level of consensus based on the literature review and validated our assessment through our expert interviews. However, anthropology was an exception and was not used in this way. As mentioned in Chapter One, because cultural anthropologists generally do not pursue consensus about variables or causal factors, we derived consensus most often from the sociology and political science literature. We used anthropology debates primarily to discuss issues lacking consensus.

Level of consensus is expressed as strong/pronounced agreement, moderate agreement/ some disagreement, and strong/pronounced disagreement:

- **Strong/pronounced agreement:** Multiple reputable, high-quality sources (i.e., academic or research/policy products) indicate that a factor plays a role in instigating or perpetuating a violence-prone environment. Any disagreement in the literature about relevance of this factor is outside the mainstream of debate.
- **Moderate agreement/some disagreement:** There is general agreement that this factor plays a role in creating or maintaining violence-prone environments. However, there is some disagreement about how this process takes place (e.g., its applicability across conflicts or the aspects of the factor that are most important).
- **Strong/pronounced disagreement:** Reputable, high-quality sources disagree significantly over whether this factor plays a role in instigating or perpetuating a violence-prone environment.

The factor matrix in Appendix B serves as a static display that enables us to note important variables involved in a variety of conflicts. A single factor rarely, if ever, appears as the sole perpetuator or instigator of an environment susceptible to violence. Generally, several factors play a role simultaneously in a given conflict or environment and are interrelated in important ways. The presence, form, and salience of each factor influences the roles of other factors. Portraying all the interdependencies and relationships among factors is beyond the scope of this study. Thus, in this section we treat individual factors and only note a few key interrelationships. In the subsequent chapter, we look at two particular conflicts and describe how the relevant factors may have interacted to create the conditions for environments prone to conflict and COIN outcomes.

Factor 1: Level of External Support for Violent, Nonstate Groups

Overview. External support for violent, nonstate groups often plays an important role in instigating and perpetuating environments susceptible to insurgency and terrorism. A variety of studies have indicated that most important terrorist and insurgent groups benefit from state sponsorship and that state-sponsored groups tend to be more deadly.[6]

Key Aspects. Outside support is typically designed to augment the nonstate group's warfighting capacity and may include the transfer of weapons, money, intelligence, and logistical assistance.[7] However, sponsorship may begin before a nonstate group turns to violence or openly challenges the target state's police, military, or security services. Preconflict support may include the provision of controlled safe havens, "non-policed" cross-border sanctuaries, diplomatic backing, ideological direction, or political mobilization assistance in the target state. The detection of this type of support may provide "early warning" of a destabilizing environment.

Outside support typically originates from two types of sponsors—states and nonstate groups, including diaspora and refugee communities. Their motivations for providing support vary considerably. States usually provide support to weaken or destabilize an adversary government, project power, enhance their international prestige, export their political system, or satisfy a domestic political objective.[8] Diaspora communities tend to support ethnic or religious kin engaged in resisting an oppressive government. A RAND study of external support for insurgent movements noted that diaspora communities have made a significant impact on rebel groups since the end of the Cold War and are currently positioned to make an even larger impact.[9]

Mitigating Variables. The external support factor is mitigated by several key variables. The most important are the extent and type of the outside support. Interestingly, more support may not always be better for the nonstate group in the long term—a group that becomes highly dependent on support may collapse when assistance is reduced or terminated. The motivation of the external sponsor is also a critical mitigating variable. In some cases, the sponsor may manipulate and undermine the capacity of the nonstate group in order to "decommission" or control it more effectively.[10] Finally, external support for combatants from neighboring countries (e.g., Iran in Afghanistan) has different consequences than support from afar—for instance, allowing cross-border safe havens.

Conflict Examples. Contemporary examples of external sponsorship of irregular warriors include Iran's support for Hezbollah, Pakistan's support for Lashkar-e-Tayyiba and the Haqqani Taliban, and the Somali diaspora's support for al-Shabbab fighters in the Horn of Africa. Historical examples of outside support include Libya's support for the Irish Republican Army, Liberia's support for the Revolutionary United Front in Sierra Leone, and Greece's support for the Kurdistan Workers' Party.

---

[6] See, for example, Ben Connable and Martin Libicki, *How Insurgencies End*, Santa Monica, Calif.: RAND Corporation, MG-965-MCIA, 2010; Daniel Byman, *Deadly Connections: States That Sponsor Terrorism*, New York: Cambridge University Press, 2005; Chris Quillen, "A Historical Analysis of Mass Casualty Bombers," *Studies in Conflict and Terrorism*, Vol. 25, No. 5, 2002; and Daniel Byman, Peter Chalk, Bruce Hoffman, William Rosenau, and David Brannan, *Trends in Outside Support for Insurgent Movements*, Santa Monica, Calif.: RAND Corporation, MR-1405-OTI, 2001.

[7] Byman, 2005.

[8] Byman, 2005.

[9] Byman et al., 2001.

[10] Daniel Byman, *Understanding Proto-Insurgencies*, Santa Monica, Calif.: RAND Corporation, OP-178-OSD, 2007.

Level of Consensus. There is strong agreement in the literature for this factor, particularly among political scientists. Several comprehensive political science reviews of the insurgency and terrorism literature, including Davis and Cragin (2009), have highlighted the significant attention devoted to this factor and the nearly universal agreement about its importance.[11]

Sociologists and anthropologists have devoted less attention directly to this issue, but numerous studies from these fields have shown the importance of closely related phenomena, including the critical role of resource mobilization in social movements and the role of external linkages in tribally based insurgent networks.[12]

Factor 2: Extent to Which Government Considered Illegitimate or Ineffective by the Population

Overview. Government is perceived to be unrepresentative by the population and perceived to be failing to provide basic services. This is typically found in states where a political elite benefits economically, but the mass population is relatively deprived by comparison. Perceived illegitimacy and ineffectiveness are both considered within this factor, since both are defined by local expectations about maintaining order, delivering services, and other expected government functions.

Key Aspects. In order for a violent nonstate or insurgent group to arise, it must have (1) opportunity and (2) cause. One factor contributing to both opportunity and cause is whether the local population perceives the ruling government to be illegitimate or does not distribute resources or social service equitably, causing disgruntlement and undermining the legitimacy of the government.[13] States with capacity gaps tend to develop functional holes (that is, they are unable to carry out the normal functions of the modern state) that offer opportunities to nonstate actors. In some cases, these actors simply exploit the permissive space created by such functional holes as the lack of effective criminal justice; in others, they become the proxy for the state, thereby further challenging its authority and legitimacy.[14] Weak and failed states are at great risk of becoming havens for transnational terrorist and guerrilla groups. Lack of enforcement capabilities enables militant organizations to infiltrate and fill the "vacuum of power" that is created in the absence of a strong state (see also Factor 6: Existence of Ungoverned Space for discussion of the absence of state infrastructure and social services).

Notably, if government cannot provide sufficient security, justice, or access to resources on an individual level, familial bonds will continue to present the most effective means of local governance and morality. This will lead to resource hoarding and the perpetuation of conflict, as well as block efforts at state-building and centralized stabilization.[15]

Mitigating Variables. One mitigating variable that affects the extent to which the local population considers the government to be illegitimate or ineffective is the concentration of

---

[11] Davis and Cragin, 2009; James Fearon and David Laitin, "Ethnicity, Insurgency, and Civil War," *American Political Science Review*, Vol. 97, No. 1, February 2003; and Weinstein, 2006.

[12] McCarthy and Zald, 1977; Charles Tilly, *Social Movements, 1768–2004*, Boulder, Colo.: Paradigm Publishers, 2004; and David Kilcullen, *Counterinsurgency*, New York: Oxford University Press, 2010.

[13] J. Bernhard Compton, "Violent Non-State Actors in the Middle Eastern Region," *Small Wars Journal*, 2008; and Phil Williams, *Violent Non-State Actors and National and International Security*, Zurich, Switzerland: International Relations and Security Network, 2008.

[14] Williams, 2008.

[15] Simons, 1997.

popular discontent: Is it localized in certain regions of a state, or within one group of the population? Another variable is the effectiveness and strength of government security services to perpetuate political inequalities.[16] Finally, the extent to which violent, nonstate groups are able to leverage and perpetuate a local population's grievances with the state determines the salience of this factor. There must be some sort of catalyst to mobilize an identity group, possibly transforming it into a full-fledged violent nonstate actor group. An "identity entrepreneur" who creates or reinforces the identity that now stands opposed to the state typically provides this catalyst.[17] The more successful these identity entrepreneurs, the more followers they have (see Factor 9).

Conflict Examples. A number of examples highlight how this factor has been a contributing force to insurgency. For example, the Palestinian Liberation Organization (PLO) in the 1970s and 1980s, Hezbollah in Lebanon since 1982, the Rwandan Hutu Interahamwe (operating in Zaire), and the Nicaraguan Contras (operating in Honduras) all capitalized on and exploited a popular sense of government illegitimacy or ineffectiveness.[18]

Level of Consensus. There is strong agreement that this factor is salient in the production and maintenance of unstable, violence-prone environments over time.

Factor 3: Presence of Tribal or Ethnic Indigenous Populations with History of Resisting State Rule, and/or Cultures That Encourage or Justify Violent Behavior

Overview. This factor includes two different cultural patterns: (1) a proclivity toward intensely localized social organization and government (i.e., ignoring or resisting central governance) and (2) the normalization, justification, and sometimes glorification of violence as a proper means of resolving disputes. Both patterns involve some degree of local historical and social inertia—that is, groups develop these patterns over time and they are therefore difficult to change quickly.

Key Aspects. Patterns of evading or resisting centralized state rule are central themes in this factor. Also critical is the fact that such groups tend to inhabit forbidding or hard-to-reach locations in places in which it is impractical for governments to maintain a steady or frequent presence. Finally, such groups have evolved a relatively autonomous, nonhierarchical way of resolving disputes and making decisions, and they both resent and resist attempts to overturn or subsume these relatively flat systems of social regulation and control by a central governing authority. James C. Scott (2009) has written extensively on groups and cultures that have evolved a pattern of evading or resisting centralized state rule, with his foremost work concerning the highlands of Southeast Asia.[19] Critical to Scott's argument is how these groups have adopted ways of making a living that are both hard to track and do not involve dependence on specific, designated tracts of land (for example, herding agriculture). The "culture of violence" argument has also received considerable attention from scholars of aggression and warfare. Anthropologists have noted group differences in the acceptance of violence and aggression as

---

[16] Davis and Cragin, 2009.

[17] Michael J. Mazarr, "The Psychological Sources of Islamic Terrorism: Alienation and Identity in the Arab World," Hoover.org/Policy Review, No. 125, Stanford University, June 1, 2004.

[18] Boaz Atzili, "State Weakness and 'Vacuum of Power' in Lebanon," *Terrorism,* Vol. 33, No. 8, 2010, pp. 757–782; and Austin T. Turk, "Sociology of Terrorism," *Annual Review of Sociology,* Vol. 30, No. 1, 2004, pp. 271–286.

[19] Scott, 2009.

a means of interacting with others in villages only a short distance away from each other.[20] Violence as a way of life is often trained early, such as in the rituals of manhood practiced by tribes in Papua New Guinea.[21] In certain environments, violence may also be glorified (and the population desensitized to its effects) through immersive exposure in media that contain gruesome images of the aftermath of violent attacks or the "excitement" of the attack itself. Literature on the Palestinian Occupied Territories describes both a kind of ritual exposure to violence and the glorification and justification of violence through both popular images (e.g., martyrdom videos and posters) advertising the efforts and gruesome impact of suicide bombers and through incorporation into religious notions.[22] Meanwhile, Keiser's work describes how cultures of blood feuds and vengeance become part of cultural systems that invoke and channel fundamental human emotions and motivations.[23]

Mitigating Variables. One important mitigating variable pertaining to groups with a history of resisting state rule is the capacity of the state to extend monitoring, infrastructure, and control to remote locations and formerly untracked forms of livelihood or trade. Another mitigating variable is the degree to which these groups are willing to make sacrifices to maintain their autonomy and way of life, or that some elements of the group might be tempted to assimilate into a national or state-regulated way of life.

With respect to cultures of violence, it is important to consider the means by which violence is made to seem an acceptable mode of action. That is, does this happen through ritual violence during major life transitions? Is it inculcated through exposure to targeted forms of radical violent media? Some of these particular social exposures may be amenable to intervention, although violence generally tends to be socialized through a variety of social mechanisms acting in concert. The justification of violence is also often centered on key events in historical memory and the narratives that surround them. While intervening in these established narratives of identity may be particularly difficult, it may be possible to shape or reinterpret aspects of these narratives in more nonviolent directions.

Conflict Examples. Scott describes historical examples of small groups and cultures resisting state rule across the highlands of Southeast Asia,[24] and Barfield describes Afghanistan as a similar case, particularly with respect to rule of law.[25] As noted above, researchers have noted how violence pervades the cultural and media context in the Palestinian Occupied Territories, particularly during the height of the Second Intifada.[26] Similarly, both the separatist movement in Chechnya[27] and the Sandinistas in El Salvador[28] have been described as helping to mobilize and create a "culture of violence" in each respective region, partially through their

---

[20] Fry, 1992.

[21] Tuzin, 1982.

[22] Allen, 2008.

[23] R. Lincoln Keiser, "Death Enmity in Thull: Organized Vengeance and Social Change in a Kohistani Community," *American Ethnologist*, Vol. 13, No. 3, 1986, pp. 489–505.

[24] Scott, 2009.

[25] Barfield, 2008.

[26] Allen, 2008.

[27] H. Johnston, "Ritual, Strategy, and Deep Culture in the Chechen National Movement," *Critical Studies on Terrorism*, Vol. 1, No. 3, 2008, pp. 321–342.

[28] P. Bourgois, "The Power of Violence in War and Peace," *Ethnography*, Vol. 2, No. 1, 2001, pp. 5–34.

provocation of state responses. Williams makes similar arguments about how culture contributes to violence in 21st-century Mexico and Iraq.[29]

Level of Consensus. There is strong disagreement in the literature regarding this factor. This is due to the fact that there is significant debate in the literature regarding the degree to which these cultural patterns are inherently bound to specific groups or are due to the influence of social context. Much of this debate centers on scholars' hesitance to designate a particular cultural group as having a "culture of violence" or a "culture of resistance" at its essential core and instead to prefer historical contextual explanations for why violence arises and persists in certain groups and movements. For one example of such a debate, see Binford's arguments against Bourgois's designation of El Salvador as having a "culture of violence."[30]

Factor 4: Levels of Absolute or Relative Poverty/Inequality; Presence of One or More Groups That Have Recently Lost Status or Power

Overview. This factor refers to the degree to which absolute poverty or destitution, relative differences in wealth across subgroups, or recent changes in the social status or power of different subgroups contribute to instability and conflict.

Key Aspects. There are several pathways by which scholars have suggested that this factor contributes to instability. The first is that poor or destitute individuals might be more vulnerable to real or promised financial incentives from nonstate actors. For example, promises of wealth distributions to families of suicide bombers in the Palestinian Occupied Territories have purportedly helped incentivize would-be bombers.[31] Similarly, financial incentives help motivate rural Afghans to provide part-time operational assistance to the Taliban, especially when times are tough.[32] It has also been suggested that poverty and destitution contribute to instability by lowering perceived future life chances and thereby creating a general increase in violent and risk-taking tendencies within a population (a "devil-may-care" attitude)—effectively increasing the pool of possible combatants or criminals in a population.[33] Disenfranchised groups, even within otherwise stable stages, present a ready source of foot soldiers.[34]

A second line of thought with respect to this factor concerns itself with whether certain subgroups in a population perceive the distribution of wealth or power to be unjust. That is, there is noticeable inequality in access to resources or political power that falls along ethnic, tribal, or even clan or familial lines that a group feels is an inequitable situation and needs to be rectified. This can be particularly powerful if relatively recent changes in the distribution of wealth or power have taken place. A well-known historical case of this is the Rwandan genocide, in which the once-elite class of minority Tutsis and newly empowered Hutus engaged in years of massacres.[35]

[29] Phil Williams, "Illicit Markets, Weak States and Violence: Iraq and Mexico," *Crime, Law and Social Change*, Vol. 52, No. 3, 2009, pp. 323–336.

[30] L. Binford, "Violence in El Salvador," *Ethnography*, Vol. 3, No. 2, 2002, pp. 201–219.

[31] Council on Foreign Relations, "Backgrounder: Hamas," Web page, October 20, 2011.

[32] R. Hanlin, "One Team's Approach to VSO," *Small Wars Journal*, Vol. 7, No. 9, 2011, pp. 1–8.

[33] J. S. Chisholm, *Death, Hope and Sex: Steps to an Evolutionary Ecology of Mind and Morality*, New York: Cambridge University Press, 1999.

[34] Simons and Tucker, 2007.

[35] Human Rights Watch, *Leave None to Tell the Story*, HRW Legacy Reports, 1999.

Mitigating Variables. One mitigating variable that enables poverty and destitution to be linked to instability is the set of financial incentives that a nonstate actor has developed to mobilize action. For example, the Taliban in Afghanistan have successfully exploited a strategy of providing financial incentives to join their efforts by offering payments for informing, conducting small tasks (such as emplacing jugs of homemade explosive), or even part-time involvement in direct fire attacks.

A key mitigating variable for inequality is the degree to which cultural belief systems justify (or decry) the inequitable distribution of wealth, privilege, and power. For example, connections between royalty and religious institutions (e.g., the "Church" or the "Mosque") historically have created mass idolization of royal lineages. Kings in Saudi Arabia (as Custodians of the Two Holy Mosques), Jordan (as direct descendants of the Prophet Muhammad), and Thailand (as defenders of Buddhism) have helped maintain social order for years, although the social contracts in those countries have frayed at times in recent history. In contrast, the arrival and popularization of liberation theology in Latin America helped mobilize multiple insurgencies and guerrilla movements.[36] Ideological systems (and their use by nonstate actors) that decry the inequitable distribution of wealth are power are critical for enabling inequality to be used as a catalyst for social mobilization and violence.

Conflict Examples. As mentioned above, the Palestinian Occupied Territories, Afghanistan, multiple conflicts in Latin America, and the Rwandan genocide have all been mentioned with respect to the role of poverty and inequality in causing instability. Additionally, the Ba'athists in Iraq represent a group that lost status and power and mobilized an insurgency partially to rectify their losses and attempt to regain power.

Level of Consensus. There is moderate agreement in the literature regarding the role of relative deprivation and perceived injustices of inequality in causing instability and leading to violent environments. It is well accepted that group-level differences in wealth or power are frequent themes that revolutionary or genocidal social movements capitalize on to mobilize individuals to violence.

Furthermore, while the link between absolute poverty or income inequality and violent *crime* is quite well established,[37] criminal activity alone does not necessarily lead to levels of instability that prompt insurgency or social movements. The link between poverty alone and terrorist recruits, in particular, has come into question through a series of careful analyses in multiple theaters. While many still argue that absolute poverty plays a role, the data suggest that the relationship between poverty and involvement in terrorism either is not strong or is the opposite of expectations. That is, wealthier or better-educated individuals, and not the undereducated or the poor, are more involved in insurgency activities.[38]

---

[36] T. X. Hammes, "War Evolves into the Fourth Generation," *Contemporary Security Policy*, Vol. 26, No. 2, 2005, pp. 189–221.

[37] C. Hsieh and M. D. Pugh, "Poverty, Income Inequality, and Violent Crime: A Meta-Analysis of Recent Aggregate Data Studies," *Criminal Justice Review*, Vol. 18, No. 2, 1993, pp. 182–202.

[38] A. B. Krueger and J. Maleckova, *Education, Poverty, Political Violence, and Terrorism: Is There a Causal Connection?* Cambridge, Mass.: National Bureau of Economic Research Working Papers, 2002.

Factor 5: Extent to Which Local Governance Is Fragmented or Nonexistent and Vulnerable to Co-Option from Insurgent Replacement Institutions

Overview. In some unstable environments, local systems for the provision of schooling, health care, dispute resolution, group decisionmaking, or other services either are very rudimentary or insufficient, have recently broken down, or can be pushed aside through coercion or intimidation by nonstate actors. One way for insurgent groups to take and hold ground is to fill this civil governance gap by providing schooling (even if radicalized and ideological), health care, rule of law, or other services. This helps garner the allegiance and support of the local populace and also serves an information operations (IO) role.

Key Aspects. Of critical importance in this factor is the degree to which local social and governance systems have been eroded, as well as the fragility and vulnerability of the local population (i.e., the local "need" for social services). A closely related factor is the presence of ungoverned space (see Factor 6), as a key component of government is often the provision of basic social services.[39] Another related factor is the capacity of nonstate groups (see Factor 11), which determines the type and degree of social services that can be provided to the local population. Yet another closely related factor is the degree to which the government is perceived to be illegitimate or ineffective (see Factor 2), although this factor focuses more directly on the functioning of individual state institutions rather than the government's overall perception by the population. Terrorist and insurgent groups often fill gaps in social services strategically for both public relations reasons and to garner local allegiance, such as when al Qaeda made a public announcement of its intention to provide disaster assistance to Pakistan after the 2010 floods and al Qaeda–linked organizations subsequently provided such assistance.

Afghanistan represents a case in point for this factor. In Afghanistan, the Taliban continue to be an attractive option to locals, particularly because they provide a rudimentary sort of justice or rule of law. The Soviets worked concertedly to disable (and in some cases destroy) tribal systems of governance, assassinating key leaders and elders as part of larger intimidation campaigns. In some areas of Afghanistan, this has left a population of individuals who no longer remember how to hold shuras, jirgas, or other traditional meetings to make decisions or resolve disputes to this day. The Taliban capitalized on the lawlessness and abuses in the wake of the Soviets' defeat by taking a stand against nepotism and corruption and providing quick justice. Even after extensive efforts at state-building in the wake of removing the Taliban from Kabul, formal Afghan governance is generally not strong in remote areas. The Taliban easily fall in on this power vacuum, replacing or co-opting traditional tribal or budding regional governance with "shadow governors" and power brokers. Additionally, due to underdevelopment and below-subsistence conditions in the Afghan countryside with no social safety net, the local populace is vulnerable to financial incentives for work as a Taliban informant or even part-time combatant.

Other examples of organizations and individuals who have thrived in the relative lack of local social order include Hezbollah and Muqtada al-Sadr in Iraq.

Mitigating Variables. One critical mitigating variable is the degree to which the local population *expects* the provision of certain types of social services. It is easier for terrorist or insurgent groups to capitalize on a gap in services, governance, or rule of law if the local popu-

---

[39] Notably, some scholars prefer the term *undergoverned space* to emphasize that social order tends to emerge in local contexts even if it is not state-sanctioned or -controlled. In this report, we use the term *ungoverned* to denote lack of state presence and administration.

lation truly sees this as a gap—and especially if they believe or can be led to believe that this gap is due to state negligence, incompetence, or reneging on promises. As noted above, also critical is the absolute need of the population—for example, the poverty and destitution in the Afghan countryside or devastation in the wake of the floods in Pakistan—which increases the impact of social service efforts by nonstate actors.

Conflict Examples. As well as the examples noted above (al Qaeda in Pakistan and the Taliban in Afghanistan), two contemporary cases of insurgent organizations providing social services include Hamas in the Gaza Strip and Hezbollah in Lebanon. Hamas is estimated to spend up to 90 percent of its annual budget on the provision of social services,[40] while Hezbollah spends an estimated 50 percent of its annual budget on reconstruction, educational scholarships, and the like—and connects such charitable behavior with Muslim notions of duty or "zakat."[41]

Level of Consensus. There is strong agreement in the literature about the salience of this factor for unstable environments. It is generally agreed that providing social services to the local population (when it occurs) is important in generating and maintaining support for nonstate actors.[42] Part of this importance may lie in the fact that homegrown insurgent movements often operate directly in places that the state finds harder to reach and therefore know the grievances, needs, and concerns of these populations better than anyone else. This also seems to be a popular tactic in Islamic organizations because of the connection between charity toward other Muslims and shared religious values. However, not all nonstate actors engage in the provision of social services.

Factor 6: Existence of Ungoverned Space

Overview. Ungoverned space often plays a role in perpetuating unstable environments. While not all ungoverned spaces develop into environments that feed insurgency or terrorism, many such conflicts are sustained by ungoverned space.

Key Aspects. Ungoverned territory, characterized by a lack of state penetration, physical infrastructure, monopoly on the use of force, and border controls, may develop for a variety of reasons. The state may not have sufficient resources to extend its reach to remote regions or to challenge nonstate groups for dominance in ethnic, tribal, or political enclaves.[43] Failed states are breeding grounds for the practice and innovation of terrorist tactics, but they are not always the best safe havens (there is a cost to providing security in chaotic environments). Many terrorists come from otherwise stable states but may feel themselves to be disenfranchised.[44]

Some ungoverned spaces are more conducive to insurgency and terrorism than others. Rabasa and others found that ungoverned territories with adequate infrastructure for movement and communication had a higher risk of being exploited by violent groups. Vinci asserts that financially motivated warlords develop most readily where governance is very weak, but

---

[40] Council on Foreign Relations, 2011.

[41] M. J. B. Love, *Hezbollah: A Charitable Revolution*, School of Advanced Military Studies Monographs, Fort Leavenworth, Kan.: U.S. Army School of Advanced Military Studies, 2008.

[42] Davis and Cragin, 2009, p. 141.

[43] Angel Rabasa, Steven Boraz, Peter Chalk, Kim Cragin, Theodore Karasik, Jennifer Moroney, Kevin O'Brien, and John Peters, *Ungoverned Territories: Understanding and Reducing Terrorism Risks*, Santa Monica, Calif.: RAND Corporation, MG-561-AF, 2007, pp. 29–32.

[44] Simons and Tucker, 2007.

not yet absent.[45] Violent extremists may be particularly likely to gain traction where inhabitants of ungoverned territory are frustrated with the government's lack of services. In these circumstances, ungoverned space can play a role in the instigation of an unstable environment prone to sustainment of such groups.

In some circumstances, the ungovernability of a territory is both a resource and a desired outcome for a nonstate group. A nonstate group may cultivate a particular ungoverned space to develop its insurgency, which renders the space even more ungovernable and, as a result, solidifies the nonstate group's hold on it. This is a common technique for terrorist movements—as Martha Crenshaw noted, terrorism is "often designed to disrupt and discredit the processes of government."[46]

Mitigating Variables. Key mitigating variables for this factor include the strength of government military and security forces and the strength and commitment of outside forces supporting the government. Especially in difficult or underpopulated terrain, the government requires more resources and manpower to monitor and govern hard-to-reach areas. Weather, aggressive criminal elements, a nonsupportive local population, and other factors can all create logistical barriers to monitoring certain areas and thereby create more ungoverned space. Finally, the availability of exploitable natural resources, communications, and transportation infrastructure creates "attractors" for rival groups to target areas and exploit these resources, making them more difficult to protect by government forces—especially if such forces are stretched thin or concentrated in other parts of the country.[47]

Conflict Examples. Contemporary examples of violent actors exploiting ungoverned spaces include separatists in Yemen and drug trafficking groups on the Guatemalan-Mexican frontier, as well as insurgent and criminal groups in remote areas of Afghanistan and Pakistan. Southern Afghanistan is a classic example of this issue. It is rugged and mountainous and has forbidding weather, including scorching hot summers and torrential, flooding rains in the winter. The population concentration is low and, at best, neutral with respect to the central government. Finally, the availability of a lucrative opium crop in the region both attracts violent criminal elements and provides an attractive local resource for exploitation by insurgent groups. Historical examples include the Egyptian Islamic Group in central Egypt and Islamic militants in the Indonesian province of Central Sulawesi.

Level of Consensus. There is strong agreement in the literature that ungoverned territory frequently serves to perpetuate insurgency and terrorism. Many studies highlight this finding by focusing on subtypes of conflict. Fearon and Laitin, for example, found that the likelihood of experiencing a civil war or rebellion is directly related to the ungovernability of a territory.[48]

Factor 7: Presence of Multiple Violent, Nonstate Groups Competing for Power

Overview. An unstable environment leading to armed intervention is of course more likely to develop in countries that contain many violent or radicalized nonstate groups compet-

---

[45] Anthony Vinci, "A Conceptual Analysis of Warlords," *Review of African Political Economy*, Vol. 34, No. 112, June 2007.

[46] Martha Crenshaw, "The Causes of Terrorism," *Comparative Politics*, Vol. 13, No. 4, July 1981.

[47] See Robert D. Lamb, "Ungoverned Areas and Threats from Safe Havens," Washington, D.C.: Office of the Under Secretary of Defense for Policy, DTIC Document ADA479805, 2008.

[48] Fearon and Laitin, 2003.

ing for power.[49] State "failure" is an important aspect of this variable: Where groups compete violently to achieve their political, social, or economic goals, it is likely that the government is absent, overpowered, or actively supporting one or several groups. In some respects, the presence of violent, competing groups is an indicator that irregular war is already being waged.

Key Aspects. Competing, violent groups may have tribal, ethnic, social, or political roots. They are more likely to develop in places where the government is unable or unwilling to curtail their activities, creating important linkages between this factor and the "ungoverned spaces" factor. Rabasa and others argue that "the presence of extremist groups or communities vulnerable to co-option" and "a preexisting state of violence or ethno-religious cleavages that could be engineered to fit with extremist agendas" make ungoverned territories particularly attractive to insurgents.[50]

Competing groups may also co-evolve their violent tactics and capabilities as they learn from targeting and evading one another. Competition will likely cause groups to invest more heavily in recruiting and, possibly, developing more-extreme radicalization schemes to attract domestic and foreign supporters and fighters.

Mitigating Variables. Key mitigating variables for this factor include the number of competing, violent groups in an area of operations, the extent to which each of the groups are in conflict with one another, the capabilities and intentions of each of the groups, and the extent to which the groups have centers of gravity that can be attacked or disrupted.

Conflict Examples. Contemporary examples of competing, violent groups include drug traffickers in northern Mexico and militants battling in the FATA in Pakistan. Historical examples include drug trafficking and insurgent groups in Colombia in the 1990s and terrorist and criminal groups in Northern Ireland in the 1980s.

Level of Consensus. There is a moderate agreement in the literature regarding the salience of this factor. A 2009 RAND review of the counterterrorism literature noted a consensus on the importance of "radicalizing social groups" and "mobilizing structures" in terrorist group formation.[51] Radicalizing social groups and preexisting mobilization structures are common features of an environment marked by competing, violent groups. Sociologists and anthropologists have devoted significantly less attention directly to this issue, although numerous sociological studies of violent youth gangs cite the importance of radicalizing social groups in the instigation and perpetuation of violence.[52]

Factor 8: Level of Government Restriction on Political or Ideological Dissent; Extent to Which Individuals Feel Alienated from Governing Process

Overview. Individuals who are disappointed that they are not able to participate fully in political life and recognize political inequalities (such as those with higher incomes or young

---

[49] In some environments, radical, but nonviolent, political groups have refrained from violently challenging the government or one another until a key flashpoint precipitates such conflict.

[50] Rabasa et al., 2007.

[51] Davis and Cragin, 2009, pp. 74–77.

[52] Malcolm W. Klein, *The American Street Gang: Its Nature, Prevalence, and Control*, Oxford, UK: Oxford University Press, 1995; Joan Moore, Diego Vigil, and Robert Garcia, "Residence and Territoriality in Chicano Gangs," *Social Problems*, Vol. 31, No. 2, December 1983; James Diego Vigil, "Urban Violence and Street Gangs," *Annual Review of Anthropology*, Vol. 32, 2003, pp. 225–242; and Roy L. Austin, "Adolescent Subcultures of Violence," *The Sociological Quarterly*, Vol. 21, No. 4, 1980, pp. 545–561.

people with high education levels) are more likely than their less advantaged counterparts to become involved in a process of radicalization moving toward violence.

Key Aspects. Strain theory and conflict theory[53] suggest that individuals who experience a mismatch between their expectations or aspirations for political involvement and the reality of a strong state apparatus that does not allow political participation (or only a limited amount) are those who are most likely to pursue a radical or violent path toward upheaval. This occurs because those individuals are blocked from achieving their economic or political goals. Political and/or economic inequalities are therefore the sources of collective violence.[54] The key to this factor is the perceived injustices or inequities, with violence being a response to oppression and exploitation.[55]

Mitigating Variables. Two mitigating variables should be considered when determining whether political oppression is a key factor in violent insurgent activity. One is the level of economic inequality within a nation or relative poverty among a local population, which can accentuate feelings of unfairness and heighten the awareness of oppression. A second is the openness of access to an education system within a country—that is, the extent to which all members of a community or country have opportunities to attend and stay in school. (This can often be measured via gross and net education, literacy rates, or educational attainment by cohorts.) Opportunity for education affects the population's awareness of oppression by the state. And third is the level of oppression, which could determine the level of risk for an insurgency. It is also critical to consider *who* feels left out of the governance processes or feels oppressed by existing governance structures. If these patterns of exclusion, alienation, or oppression map onto specific ethnic, tribal, linguistic, or other groups, then such groups could form fault lines for the mobilization of resistance to the state. In fact, insurgencies themselves have even been referred to in terms of "rhetoric of political exclusion."[56]

Conflict Examples. One example of how inequities in political participation can foment insurgency is the Revolutionary Armed Forces of Colombia (Fuerzas Armadas Revolucionarias de Colombia [FARC]), which was founded in 1966 by members of the Central Committee of the Communist Party of Colombia (Partido Comunista de Colombia [PCC]). At that time, FARC embraced PCC's Soviet-style Marxist-Leninist ideological orientation. PCC reportedly also supplied the arms and financial assistance that proved critical during the early years of FARC's organization. The early membership of FARC consisted of communist ideologues, as well as noncommunist peasants, many of whom had been active during the 1950s movement to divide Colombia into various republics. The Colombian army forcibly dismantled these republics by 1966, leaving these groups without a state-sanctioned means of expression and giving them (in their own eyes) no choice but violent revolt.

Level of Consensus. There is strong disagreement in the social science fields about the relationship between open political participation (democracy) and insurgency. One reason for this is that while there are ample examples in which political oppression has led to violent

---

[53] Collins, 1994.

[54] Fearon and Laitin, 2003.

[55] McAdam, McCarthy, and Zald, 1996; Randall Collins, *Conflict Sociology: Toward an Explanatory Science,* New York: Academic Press, 1975; Griffith, 2010; and J. Robert Lilly, Francis T. Cullen, and Richard A. Ball, *Criminology Theory: Context and Consequences,* Thousand Oaks, Calif.: Sage Publications, 2007.

[56] Simons, 1999.

uprisings, there are also examples worldwide in which a lack of access to political opportunities or institutionalized barriers to political participation has not led to insurgency. For example, this is the case in countless strong dictatorial regimes throughout history, such as North Korea in the present day. Meanwhile, the caste system has existed in India for centuries with only very few, isolated incidents of caste-driven violence.

Factor 9: Level of Consistency/Agreement Between Nonstate Group's Goals and Philosophy and Preferences/Worldview/Ideology of Target Populations

Overview. This factor refers to the ability of insurgent, terrorist, and other nonstate groups to utilize or develop symbols, narratives, and an overall appeal that accords with the local population's sense of identity, morality, and general understanding of the world. This capacity is essential for the recruitment of support and personnel and helps such groups win strategic battles both within their area of operations and with external supporters.

Key Aspects. Successful nonstate actors often connect with the values, beliefs, and moral systems of local populations. In doing so, these groups capitalize on preexisting beliefs and values in the population but may also manipulate these to create new forms of identity or understandings. Over time, allegiance to these organizations—or their ideological tenets or practices—may become enmeshed in local ways of life. Williams provides a pithy example of this in the way that he describes how escalating violence among Mexican drug trafficking groups both draws from and contributes to a culture of violent *machismo* in Mexico.[57] In this way, nonstate groups and their exploits often make their way into popular cultural themes, as evidenced by the pervasive popularity of the Mexican narco-ballad.

Similarly, Kilcullen describes how insurgent groups in the Islamic world capitalize on and manipulate Islamic tenets and beliefs for recruitment and support of their activities. Often, these recruitment strategies and outreach take an oppositional tone and highlight ingroup/outgroup differences, creating and capitalizing on a sense of existential fear.[58] For example, Taliban information operations in Afghanistan attempt to create a sense that coalition forces want to fundamentally change the Afghan way of life and violate the sanctity of Afghan and Muslim traditions and people. In sum, key elements of this factor include the ability of nonstate actors to target, accentuate, and manipulate local fears, grievances, value systems, cultural taboos, and core elements of identity.

Mitigating Variables. In certain scenarios (especially of the counterinsurgent variety), multiple actors are competing for cultural buy-in. Thus, the degree to which insurgent, terrorist, organized criminal, or other groups are able to obtain this buy-in depends partially on the counternarrative produced by opposing forces. Creative IO campaigns can point out cultural taboos violated by nonstate groups, such as the Taliban carrying out attacks that kill innocent Muslims during Ramadan. Another important mitigating variable is the degree of residential, historical, and cultural overlap between a nonstate group and particular population. "Homegrown" movements, especially those with a long history of residence within a community, are best positioned to capitalize on local cultural sensibilities, including local grievances, biases, and forms of identity.

---

[57] Williams, 2009.

[58] Kilcullen, 2009.

Conflict Examples. As well as the examples of Mexico and Afghanistan cited above, recent scholarship has described how Somali piracy is enmeshed within local culture to such an extent that public sympathy for pirates remains high. For example, Somali pirates redistribute much of the wealth from their exploits and defer to clan authorities in many cases. For many Somalis, piracy also represents what they sense is legitimate revenge for fishing and toxic dumping off of Somalia's shores by other countries—in other words, legitimate and even nationalistic acts of vengeance.[59]

Level of Consensus. There is strong agreement in the literature regarding the importance of insurgent or other nonstate actors' connection with the cultural sensibilities of the local population to recruit foot soldiers and maintain material and other support. However, it is worth noting that there is considerable controversy about the singular importance of Islam in making this cultural resonance between nonstate actors and the population a particularly powerful galvanizer for radicalism, violence, and instability. That is, some authors argue that Islam itself represents an inherently dangerous or destabilizing ideology.[60] Other authors (including our group) argue that when one takes a broad historical perspective, it becomes clear that many different ideological perspectives and forms of identity can be galvanized to create terrorist capabilities and activities.

Factor 10: Extent to Which Population and Nonstate Groups Perceive Faltering Government Commitment to a Counterinsurgency Campaign

Overview. The perception of level of resolve, agreement, or commitment by a local government and external supporters (e.g., another country or global entity, such as the North Atlantic Treaty Organization [NATO]) for pursuing a long-term, focused campaign against insurgent groups can affect local cost-benefit analyses of whom to support. In other words, local populations will "bandwagon" whichever group seems to hold the most conviction or resolve, whether that be the insurgency or the local government already in power.

Key Aspects. According to rational choice theory and exchange theory, individuals' actions are fundamentally "rational" in character, and people calculate the likely costs and benefits of any action before deciding what to do. In the context of this factor, insurgents are strategic actors who respond rationally to the expected probability of faltering commitment of a local government.[61] Any sign of weakness or faltering is met by emboldened attitudes, which could, in turn, lead to more violent action.[62]

Mitigating Variables. The population's access to media (or other information) that conveys the level of local government and supporters' resolve or commitment, the accuracy and

---

[59] R. Marchal, "Somali Piracy: The Local Contexts of an International Obsession," *Humanity*, Spring 2011, pp. 31–50.

[60] S. P. Huntington, *The Clash of Civilizations and the Remaking of World Order*, New York: Simon & Schuster, 1996; and Juergensmeyer, 2003.

[61] James Fearon, "Rationalist Explanations for War," *International Organization*, Vol. 49, No. 3, 1995, pp. 379–414; Christopher Fettweis, "America's Dangerous Obsession: Credibility and the War on Terror," *Political Science Quarterly*, Vol. 122, No. 4, 2007–2008, pp. 607–633; and Ehud Sprinzak, "Rational Fanatics," *Foreign Policy*, Vol. 120, 2000, pp. 66–74.

[62] James Coleman, *Foundations of Social Theory*, Cambridge, UK: Belknap, 1990; Radha Iyengar and Jonathan Monten, "Is There an 'Emboldenment' Effect? Evidence from the Insurgency in Iraq," NBER Working Paper No. 13839, May 2008; John Scott, "Rational Choice Theory," in G. Browning, A. Halcli, and F. Webster, eds., *Understanding Contemporary Society: Theories of the Present*, Thousand Oaks, Calif.: Sage Publications, 2000; and Eli Berman, Michael Callen, Joseph H. Felter, and Jacob N. Shapiro, *Do Working Men Rebel? Insurgency and Unemployment in Iraq and the Philippines*, Cambridge, Mass.: National Bureau of Economic Research, Working Paper 15547, November 2009.

credibility of the media to which the population has access, and the elasticity of the insurgents' or terrorists' perception of the adversaries' level of resolve are all mitigating variables.

Conflict Examples. In a case study of Iraqi insurgent attacks over the course of a year, researchers found that in periods after a spike in statements that were critical of the war being waged by the local government and the United States against local insurgents, insurgent attacks increased by 7–10 percent, but this effect dissipated within a month. Additionally, they found that insurgents shifted attacks from Iraqi civilian to U.S. military targets following new information about the United States' sensitivity to costs, resulting in more U.S. fatalities but fewer deaths overall. These results suggest that there is a small but measurable cost to open public debate in the form of higher attacks in the short term, and that Iraqi insurgent organizations—even those motivated by religious or ideological goals—are strategic actors that respond rationally to the expected probability of U.S. withdrawal.[63]

Level of Consensus. There is generally strong agreement about the importance of demonstrating resolve to COIN and counterterrorism. Anecdotally, there has been much concern, for example, about timetables for withdrawal galvanizing insurgent groups. However, this factor is generally not considered explicitly in anthropological or sociological analyses of successful COIN campaigns.

Factor 11: Capacity, Resources, and Expertise of Violent, Nonstate Groups

Overview. Naturally, the capacity of nonstate groups significantly shapes the character and duration of violent extremism. Highly capable groups will be more likely to initiate and sustain violent campaigns against central authority but may also draw more attention from government security and intelligence services in the early phases of conflict.

Key Aspects. A group's capacity includes its financial and human capital, technical skills and expertise, ability to adapt, ability to connect with the local population for recruitment and support, resilience to attack, and counterintelligence capabilities, which include its ability to keep personnel, plans, and activities hidden from its adversaries. A group may build its capacity internally with independent sources of income and native expertise, or it may rely on outside support to enhance its capacity and resources. For this reason, this factor is closely associated with the "external support" factor (Factor 1). A state sponsor's provision of weapons, money, intelligence, and logistical assistance will typically enhance a group's capacity immediately, but the provision of a safe haven will, in many cases, provide an even more critical, enduring boost to capacity.

Where a group derives its resources from may play an important role in how it wages its campaign against the government. Weinstein argues that insurgencies in resource-rich environments use violence more indiscriminately and recruit soldiers more opportunistically with short-term material payoffs, relative to insurgencies in resource-poor environments.[64] Weinstein's research suggests that resource-rich insurgencies are more violent but easier to dislodge, once the group's resources are depleted.

Capacity certainly affects how fiercely and efficiently a group fights, but it may also affect whether and when a group initiates a guerrilla campaign. Claude Berrebi and Brian Jackson argue that an insurgent or terrorist group's capacity shapes its decision to engage in a cam-

---

[63] Iyengar and Monten, 2008; and Vaughn P. Shannon and Michael Dennis, "Militant Islam and the Futile Fight for Reputation," *Security Studies*, Vol. 16, No. 2, 2007, pp. 287–317.

[64] Weinstein, 2006.

paign by affecting its estimate of the risks and rewards of guerrilla activities.[65] According to one interpretation, a nonstate group is more likely to engage in violent behavior if it has a high level of skill and abundant resources and, therefore, perceives that it is more likely to succeed in its campaign.

Mitigating Variables. Group capacity is shaped by several mitigating variables, including the extent of the group's resources and expertise, the source of the group's capacity (e.g., outside sponsors, resource-rich environments, or the local population), and the vulnerability of the group's sources of capacity (e.g., the government's or state sponsor's ability to interdict or disrupt sources of expertise, funding, and training and the sustainability of the group's resources).

Conflict Examples. Contemporary high-capacity groups include the Haqqani Taliban in Afghanistan (which receives sustainment from a variety of foreign sources) and Los Zetas in Mexico. The Haqqani Taliban has developed a significant warfighting capacity with the aid of elements of the Pakistani government. The group's access to safe havens in Pakistan has played a critical role in the development of its training and recruitment programs. Los Zetas, in contrast, has developed an impressive trafficking, intelligence, and warfighting capacity as a result of its drug revenue. Capacity-strained groups include Abu Sayyaf in the Philippines and the Libyan Islamic Fighting Group (LIFG) in the Sahel region. Both of these groups have been continuously disrupted and suppressed by state adversaries in the recent past and, as a result, have not been able to invest in rebuilding their human capital and technical skills.

Level of Consensus. There is, not surprisingly, strong consensus in the literature about the importance of this factor. Sociologists highlight the importance of group capacity in the context of resource mobilization theory, which argues that social movements risk failure if they are unable to attract resources, such as money and weapons, to pursue their objectives, motivate their supporters, and pay their fighters.[66]

Factor 12: Pervasiveness of Social Networks Capable of Being Galvanized and Mobilized to Resistant Action

Overview. The use of social networks to mobilize people to violent action is another factor in the development or persistence of insurgencies. Social networks are webs of relationships formed among individuals and groups of people. Linkages among people within a network can be loosely or tightly coupled, based on the regularity of contact or feelings of bonding. Networks of social relationships create a social structure. These are tied together through specific interdependencies and common interests or dislikes. People can form social networks along a number of lines (for example, racial/ethnic, religious, age, or economic).[67] While research

---

[65] Claude Berrebi, "The Economics of Terrorism and Counterterrorism: What Matters and Is Rational-Choice Theory Helpful," in Davis and Cragin, 2009, pp. 151–202; and Brian Jackson, "Organizational Decisionmaking by Terrorist Groups," in Davis and Cragin, 2009, pp. 209–249.

[66] McCarthy and Zald, 1977; and Tilly, 2004.

[67] For more information about social network theory and social network analysis, see Granovetter, 1973; Mark Granovetter, "The Strength of Weak Ties: A Network Theory Revisited," in P. V. Marsden and N. Lin, eds., *Social Structure and Network Analysis*, Beverly Hills, Calif.: Sage Publications, 1982, pp. 105–130; John Scott, "Social Network Analysis," *Sociology*, Vol. 22, No. 1, 1988, pp. 109–127; Manuel Castells, *The Rise of the Network Society*, Oxford, UK: Blackwell Publishers, 1996; Manuel Castells, *The Power of Identity (The Information Age: Economy, Society and Culture, Volume II)*, Oxford, UK: Blackwell Publishers, 1997; and Manuel Castells, *The Network Society: A Cross-Cultural Perspective*, London, UK: Edward Elgar, 2004.

has shown that most networks are homogenous, the wider and more dispersed they become, the more heterogeneous they can be.[68] In recent years, technology has been actively used as a method to galvanize social networks and to quickly communicate plans or activities to people across broad geographic areas. (See Box 3.1 for more details on the use of social media as a tool to leverage social networks.)[69]

Key Aspects. Violent, nonstate actors leverage social networks to connect, recruit, induce "self-radicalization," and propagate their ideologies, including international outreach for support and homegrown information operations.

Mitigating Variables. One mitigating variable is the level of the local population's support or tolerance for radical or violent political messages and networking. For example, "activist" insurgencies, which rely on ideological fervor because they begin with few economic endowments, must mobilize social resources in the form of preexisting networks, ethnic identities, and norms of social solidarity to economically sustain their violent actions. These forms of insurgency are more likely to use social networking to garner support than insurgencies that are well-resourced.[70] A second variable is the level of fragmentation or split loyalties within an insurgent group, which could lead to group or subgroup differences in messaging, thereby weakening the perceived coherence of the messaging and its impact on the population as a result.

Conflict Examples. Nearly every case of insurgency or social movement relies on social networks and relationships to thrive. For example, the Sunni insurgency in Iraq utilized social networks based on kinship, common military experiences, membership in Ba'athist organizations, and other ties. Likewise, the Houthi in northern Yemen drew from long-established tribal and religious networks to gain and communicate with supporters of their rebellion against the central government.

Level of Consensus. There is strong agreement within the social science fields about the importance of the use of social networks in supporting insurgencies or conflict. However, there is strong disagreement over the degree to which social media help mobilize people to action (see Box 3.1).

Concluding Remarks

In this chapter, we presented the results of our literature review and interviews with experts in the form of 12 major factors linked with the emergence of unstable environments that are susceptible to violent insurgencies or terrorist groups. In general, agreement in the literature regarding the salience of these factors was strong. Disagreement in the literature regarding factors tended to concern (1) the degree to which factors are universally salient across conflicts or apply only in limited ways or (2) somewhat esoteric subarguments about a factor, such as the

---

[68] Peter Marsden, "Core Discussion Networks of Americans," *American Sociological Review*, Vol. 52, No. 1, 1987, pp. 122–131.

[69] Jeffrey M. Ayres, "From the Streets to the Internet," *Annals of the American Academy of Political and Social Science*, Vol. 566, 1999, pp. 132–143; and Daniel Kimmage and Kathleen Ridolfo, "Iraq's Networked Insurgents," *Foreign Policy*, October 11, 2007.

[70] Weinstein, 2006.

Box 3.1: The Use of Social Media to Leverage Social Networks

Communication media and new technologies are an important tool with which to coordinate actions, build networks, practice activism, and communicate emerging political ideals. In recent years, the use of the Internet and social media (e.g., Facebook, Twitter, text messaging, chat rooms, blogs, or message boards) has enhanced the "speed, flexibility, and global reach of information flows, allowing for communication at a distance in real time" of network-based social movements.[71] These are typically referred to as computer-supported social movements (CSSMs). Such movements operate at local, regional, and global levels, while activists move back and forth between online and offline political activity. CSSMs have the potential to transform the nature of communities, sociality, and interpersonal relations. Computer-mediated communications allow geographically fragmented communities to sustain consistent and coherent interactions across vast distances.[72] Conflicts arising from the use of network forms of organizing, strategizing, and communicating political ideologies are referred to as netwars. Many actors across the spectrum of conflict—from terrorists, guerrillas, and criminals who pose security threats to social activists who may not—are developing netwar designs and capabilities.[73]

A number of variables can mitigate the use of social media or the Internet as a tool to leverage social networks. One is the extent to which the state monitors and controls access to communication technologies and other modes of communication. If the state is able to block use of the Internet or other communication technologies, then the use of digital platforms or infrastructures as a tool for mobilization can be limited. Popular perception of the state's ability to monitor communication among group's members is also a consideration in an insurgent group's use of digital technologies.[74]

A common example of the use of social media as a tool for galvanizing popular support for insurgency is the Arab Spring of 2011. In Syria and Egypt, youth protestors used social media outlets to encourage action against the ruling governments and to connect with one another to increase participation in the movement. Another seminal case of this is the Zapatista

[71] Jeffrey S. Juris, "The New Media and Activist Networking Within Anti-Corporate Globalization Movements," *Annals of the American Academy of Political and Social Science*, Vol. 597, No. 1, 2005, pp. 189–208; W. Lance Bennett, "Communicating Global Activism," *Information, Communication & Society*, Vol. 6, No. 2, 2003a, pp. 143–168; and W. Lance Bennett, "New Media Power," in Nick Couldry and James Curran, eds., *Contesting Media Power*, Lanham, Md.: Rowman & Littlefield, 2003b.

[72] Barry Wellman, "Physical Place and Cyberplace," *International Journal of Urban and Regional Research*, Vol. 25, No. 2, 2001, pp. 227–252; Barry Wellman and Caroline Haythornthwaite, eds., *The Internet in Everyday Life*, Malden, Mass.: Blackwell, 2002; Bennett, 2003a; and Bennett, 2003b.

[73] David Ronfeldt, John Arquilla, Graham E. Fuller, and Melissa Fuller, *The Zapatista "Social Netwar" in Mexico*, Santa Monica, Calif.: RAND Corporation, MR-994, 1998; John Arquilla and David Ronfeldt, *The Advent of Netwar*, Santa Monica, Calif.: RAND Corporation, MR-789-A, 1996; John Arquilla and David Ronfelt, *Networks and Netwars: The Future of Terror, Crime, and Militancy*, Santa Monica, Calif.: RAND Corporation, MR-1382-OSD, 2001.

[74] Daniel Miller and Don Slater, *The Internet: An Ethnographic Approach*, Oxford, UK: Berg Publishers, 2000; and Peter Van Aelst and Stefaan Walgrave, "New Media, New Movements? The Role of the Internet in Shaping the 'Anti-Globalization' Movement," *Information, Communication & Society*, Vol. 5, No. 4, 2002, pp. 465–493.

Box 3.1—continued

movement in Chiapas, Mexico, in 1994, which used digital technologies to mobilize networks of previously isolated groups, communicate political messages, and promote civil disobedience against the government of Mexico in coordinated, joint actions. In January 1994, a guerrilla-like insurgency in Chiapas by the Ejército Zapatista de Liberación Nacional (Zapatista National Liberation Army [EZLN]), and the Mexican government's response to it, aroused a multitude of civil-society activists associated with human rights, indigenous rights, and other types of nongovernmental organizations (NGOs) to swarm—electronically as well as physically—from the United States, Canada, and elsewhere into Mexico City and Chiapas. There, they linked with Mexican NGOs to voice solidarity with the EZLN's demands and to press for nonviolent change.[75]

Although there are case studies of insurgent groups that have successfully used the Internet or digital technologies to sustain support or leverage social networks, there is strong disagreement within the literature and among our expert interviewees about the degree to which social media, in connecting and mobilizing popular resistance and civil disobedience, helps galvanize violent action.

relative importance of religious ideology (particularly Islam in Factor 9) or the importance of group versus individual disparities in socioeconomic status (see Factor 4).

It is important to note that factors necessarily have permeable boundaries between one another. This is due to the fact that the 12 factors do not occur in isolation from one another, but are instead part of complex, mutually dependent relationships in which factors are inherently linked. For example, the capacity of a terrorist or insurgent organization (Factor 11) may lead it to be successful in catastrophic or highly visible attacks, which in turn may increase external support and contributions (Factor 1). We now explore these interrelationships among factors in the context of two case studies.

---

[75] Thomas Olesen, *Long Distance Zapatismo*, London, UK: Zed Books, 2004; Ronfeldt et al., 1998; Harry Cleaver, *The Zapatistas and the Electronic Fabric of Struggle*, Web version, 1995; and Harry Cleaver, *Computer-Linked Social Movements and the Threat to Global Capitalism*, Web version, 1999.

CHAPTER FOUR

Relationships Among Factors: Peru and Nepal Case Studies

The 12 factors identified above are neither static nor disconnected; they change over time and interact with one another differently in specific contexts or conflicts. In this chapter, we describe how some of the factors identified might have interacted in two conflicts selected by the sponsor of this research: the Shining Path (Sendero Luminoso) in Peru and the Maoist insurgency in Nepal. This allowed us to dig deeply into the historical data on these conflicts to determine how our list of factors affected the genesis, maintenance, and resolution of each conflict. Most importantly, it allowed us to analyze the interrelationships among factors and how the overlap and interconnectedness of factors can play a role in the resolution of conflicts in favor of the state or nonstate actors.

These particular cases were selected by the study sponsor because of the sponsor's familiarity with the insurgencies as a result of recent research they had undertaken; there was no other method (e.g., type of insurgency) to the selection. The purpose of our treatment of these conflicts was not to conduct an assessment that is representative or exhaustive, but to offer lenses through which analysts can apply the factors to gain insight into interactions that worsen a conflict or hasten its conclusion.

Here, we provide two alternative ways to analyze the factors in a conflict. In the Peru case, we describe interrelationships in three phases of the conflict in which two factors played primary roles and six other factors influenced them in secondary roles. In this context, the primary factors serve as "meta-factors" that appeared in the case narrative by Paul, Clarke, and Grill (2010) to have the greatest effect on the outcome of the conflict, while the secondary factors fed the meta-factors, rather than influencing the course of the conflict independently. In the Nepal case, we use the concept of a positive feedback loop to characterize the interrelationships between three primary and four secondary factors. In characterizing the events and actions of the Peru and Nepal conflicts, we are cognizant that ours is one possible narrative determining factor salience and interaction in these conflicts. There may be more compelling narratives that would lead to differing views of factor salience.[1] The purpose here is to demon-

---

[1] The narrative method uses compelling accounts of historical events to illuminate patterns within those events and then attempts to explain them. Narrative explanations are compelling to the extent that the argument made and the narrative evidence provided is compelling. Narrative results are not falsifiable in the directly conventional sense, but they can be falsified or superseded by a more compelling narrative explanation. For more on narrative historical methods, see Andrew Abbott, "Conceptions of Time and Events in Social Science Methods: Causal and Narrative Approaches," *Historical Methods*, Vol. 23, No. 4, 1990, pp. 140–150; Ronald Aminzade, "Historical Sociology and Time," *Sociological Methods & Research*, Vol. 20, No. 4, 1992, p. 463; and Robin Stryker, "Beyond History Versus Theory: Strategic Narrative and Sociological Explanation," *Sociological Methods & Research*, Vol. 24, No. 3, 1996, pp. 304–352.

strate that the factors provide a lens through which to look at ongoing conflicts or the environments in which the conflicts might arise.

This raises a second caveat, which is that we do not differentiate between factors that lead to violence and conflict and those that sustain them. Conditions that lead to insurgencies are different from the conditions necessary to sustain them; therefore, doing things one could have done to head off an insurgency may not stop one that is already under way. In assessing the effects of factors in particular circumstances, it is important for the analyst to take care to emphasize potential differences between sources of susceptibility to and sustainment of conflict.

The Shining Path in Peru, 1980–1992

Abimael Guzman established the Shining Path as a militant Maoist group in Peru's Ayacucho highlands in the late 1960s and was its leader until his capture by the Peruvian government in 1992. Beginning as an offshoot of the Communist Party of Peru, the group turned to guerrilla warfare in 1980 in the midst of a severe economic crisis, as well as government corruption and indecision. Also in that year, Peru's military government permitted a presidential election for the first time in over a decade, bringing to power a democratic but ineffective central authority. The insurgency grew with little resistance from the government until 1982, when a state of emergency was declared and the military became involved in fighting the Shining Path. But both the guerrillas and the government pursued strategies of repression and indiscriminate violence, and the government gained neither popular support nor ground in the conflict, leading to a widely held notion among the citizenry, particularly in the highlands, that that the Shining Path would prevail. The election of President Alberto Fujimori in 1990 brought a new and more successful strategy that combined development with local defense and intelligence; Guzman's capture in 1992 broke the back of the insurgency and rendered it a much less significant, though ongoing, threat.[2]

Keeping in mind the caveat stated above, viewing the conflict through the lens of the identified environmental factors can provide some useful perspectives on insurgency and terrorism. In the case of the Shining Path in Peru, a number of anthropologically and sociologically based factors appear to have been at play. Their roles changed, as did the relationships among them, over the course of three phases of the conflict: Phase I (1980–1985), Phase II (1985–1989), and Phase III (1990–1992).[3] Two factors appear to have played a primary role in the conflict, while six others influenced the primary factors' relative strength and the outcomes of COIN efforts in each phase:

- The primary factor of the legitimacy of the government was influenced by the secondary factors of perceived government commitment, fragmenting local governance, and level of government repression.

---

[2]   Paul, Clarke, and Grill, 2010, p. 57; and Kathryn Gregory, "Backgrounder: Shining Path, Tupac Amaru," Web page, Council on Foreign Relations, August 27, 2009.

[3]   Some studies of this conflict define its phases differently; the three phases defined here serve our illustrative purposes.

- The primary factor of the capacity of the insurgent group was influenced by the secondary factors of consistency between goals, ungoverned space, and level of poverty and inequality.

Figure 4.1 represents the roles of the factors through each phase. Primary factors are boxes with white backgrounds, while secondary factors appear with gray backgrounds and arrows toward the primary factors that they influence. The color of the lines and text indicates when the factor favored the Shining Path (red) or the Peruvian government (green).

Phase I. At the start of the insurgency in 1980, the Peruvian government considered the activities of the Shining Path a local law enforcement problem, and government efforts to fight the insurgents were ineffective and seen as demonstrating a lack of commitment. At the same time, fragmented local governance resulted in a paucity of basic services, particularly in areas of insurgent activity. These factors combined to delegitimize the local and central governments in the eyes of the indigenous population of the highlands, especially when seen in the context of political infighting and indecisiveness that followed the 1980 presidential elections. By 1982, insurgent gains led the government to declare states of emergency in a growing number of Peruvian regional departments, thereby bringing the military into the fight against Shining Path guerrillas. However, the military's methods at this point in the conflict were repressive and indiscriminate, casting further doubt on the legitimacy of central authority.

The Shining Path was able to exploit the severe economic crisis and the ungoverned space that existed in the more-remote Peruvian highlands to build its capacity and set up alternate governing structures while purging local officials. It gained some support from the local peasantry by providing services, filling the political void left by an ineffective and corrupt govern-

Figure 4.1
Primary and Secondary Factors in the Peruvian Shining Path Conflict, 1980–1992

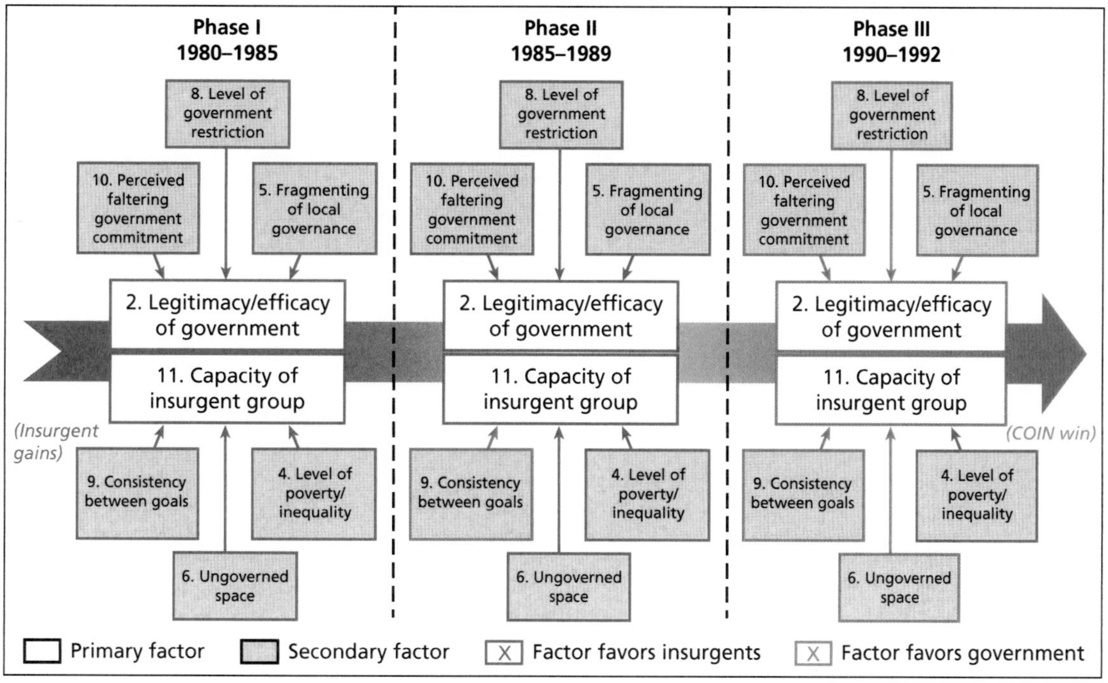

ment, and meting out popular justice against widely despised individuals.[4] The goals of the Shining Path appeared to some of the peasantry to be more supportive of their interests, in light of the perceived lack of commitment by the government. However, the guerrilla groups also gained and controlled ground through brutality, massacres, intimidation, and other forms of repression.

As a result, both primary and all six secondary factors appear in red, indicating that the factors favored the insurgents in this phase.

Phase II. Between 1985 and 1989, recognizing that the economic crisis was exacerbating the high levels of poverty in the highlands and enabling exploitation by the Shining Path, the Peruvian government instituted an investment and development strategy to improve economic conditions and job opportunities in the hardest-hit regions. However, despite an initial increase in investment and infrastructure development programs, the guerrillas effectively countered these programs, the military failed to provide the security necessary for their success, and embezzlement associated with them became common. This helped sustain the perception that the government was incompetent, corrupt, and ineffective.[5] The military, police, and intelligence services continued to use repressive tactics and torture.

The guerrillas sustained their own campaign of brutality and continued to pose a serious threat to the country's stability due to the group's strong leadership (Guzman) and organization. But their human rights abuses also alienated a large majority of Peruvians, suggesting that the group's goals and ideology did not converge with those of the local population.[6] Despite this, with the government failing to diminish ungoverned spaces and economic hardship continuing to affect the Peruvian highlands, the Shining Path remained a severe challenge and a capable insurgent group.

Thus, except for the lack of convergence between the guerrillas' goals and popular interests, the factors appeared to change very little in Phase II. Levels of government legitimacy and insurgent capacity remained in favor of the insurgents.

Phase III. In 1990, the newly elected Fujimori government pursued a new and successful strategy to combat the Shining Path that ultimately shifted the conflict in favor of the authorities. Strong emphases on development, local defense, and intelligence had the effect of both increasing the perception of government commitment to COIN and enhancing good governance in the highlands. Local civil-defense militias (or *rondas*) were a key part of this strategy. All of these actions, in addition to a strategic communication campaign and efforts to fight government corruption, helped give legitimacy to the government in the eyes of the population, particularly among citizens in Ayacucho and other departments in the highlands.[7]

During this phase, the government made headway in pushing the Shining Path out of populated areas and reducing ungoverned spaces. Moreover, the government's new strategy and continued brutality and ideological extremism by the Shining Path further alienated the local population from the group. While the government made some progress on improving

---

[4]   Commission on Truth and Reconciliation [Comisión de la Verdad y Reconciliación], Vol. VI, Chapter 1, August 23, 2003, p. 41.

[5]   Paul, Clarke, and Grill, 2010, p. 60.

[6]   Rex A. Hudson, ed., *Peru: A Country Study*, The Library of Congress, Washington, D.C.: Government Printing Office, 1992.

[7]   Paul, Clarke, and Grill, 2010, pp. 60–61.

economic conditions in the highlands, the peasantry continued to endure hardships. However, in light of other factors, this alone was not enough of a motivation for support of the insurgents. Finally, Guzman's capture in 1992 broke the back of the group;[8] Guzman's authoritarian leadership style, though effective while he was at large, left the group "decapitated" and without a galvanizing figure at its helm. The group's capacity was severely limited by the loss of its longtime leader.

The effects of the factors changed drastically during Phase III, rendering the two primary factors, government legitimacy and group capacity, in favor of the government and effectively garnering a COIN victory.[9]

The Maoist Insurgency in Nepal, 1997–2006

Nepal is an example of a budding democracy that fell prey partially to its own ineffectiveness, nepotism, corruption, and lack of governance capacity in the face of a Maoist insurgency that eventually secured a large block of power in the government. The Maoist insurgents built on a popular sense of cronyism and inefficacy on the part of the national government and used this to help secure the support of many segments of the Nepalese populace throughout the insurgency. The Nepalese government worsened these impressions of its own efficacy throughout the conflict, yielding ground in the rural areas of Nepal very quickly and never regaining control. Initial, ineffective attempts at combating the Maoists were followed by repressive, heavy-handed intervention by the Royal Army, a twin failure that both decreased the legitimacy of the national government and increased popular impressions of its inefficacy. Furthermore, the only Nepalese institution with any initial legitimacy, the Royal Family, was decimated through an apparent regicide in 2001 and the declaration of emergency rule by King Gyanendra in 2005, which both shocked and galvanized the Nepalese public to support the opposition and led to the withdrawal of international support for the central government. A broad antimonarchy coalition formed, and the Maoists secured a large block of power in the resultant resolution of the conflict.[10]

Unlike the case of the Peru, in Nepal there was no gradual betterment of conditions in favor of the central government over time. Rather, a set of initial conditions favoring popular support for the Maoists—both directly and indirectly through the delegitimization of the national government—simply got worse over time. This worsening of conditions in favor of the Maoists centered on the comparatively better military capabilities, greater popular support, and superior political savvy of the Maoist insurgency in comparison to the national government. It was fed by a series of gross missteps on the part of the national government, including an initial period of ineffective bickering and lackluster response to the insurgency, a quick loss of governance and infrastructure in the rural areas of Nepal (everywhere besides the capital of Kathmandu), and an increasingly repressive but continually ineffective military intervention.

---

[8] Guzman's capture was made possible by a government strategy focused on intelligence and local defense forces. Paul, Clarke, and Grill, 2010, p. 57.

[9] It should be noted that the Shining Path remains a threat to security in Peru, but not nearly to the extent it was prior to 1992.

[10] Paul, Clarke, and Grill, 2010, pp. 293–298.

This series of events can be pictured as a positive feedback loop, in which three primary factors were at play, fed by four secondary factors (see Figure 4.2). Just as in the case of Peru, Factors 2 (government efficacy/legitimacy) and 11 (insurgent capabilities) took center stage—not unsurprisingly, as both Nepal and Peru are classic examples of COIN conflicts. However, in the case of Nepal, the extensive ungoverned space in the Nepalese countryside (Factor 6) also played a primary role in the conflict; first because it gave the Maoists an extensive operational base, but also because the central government lost control and infrastructure across rural Nepal quickly and never managed to regain control of it (whereas the Peruvian government was able to regain control over remote rural areas). This quick loss meant that the Maoists "became the state," rapidly setting up their own shadow governance in rural areas of Nepal. This—combined with excessively repressive (and ineffective) attempts by first the police and then the Nepalese Army to combat the Maoists—quickly fed popular impressions of the inefficacy of the central government. In turn, it helped enable a resonance between popular dissatisfaction with cronyism, corruption, and inefficacy in the central government, which the Maoists capitalized on to galvanize popular support.

Over almost ten years of conflict, a positive feedback loop between Maoist capacity and effectiveness and government illegitimacy and ineffectiveness created conditions increasingly in favor of the Maoist insurgents. In contrast with the case of Peru, where government counter-insurgent efforts were able to sever interrelationships between factors contributing to the insurgency and build up suitable responses to the Shining Path, factors feeding the Maoist insurgency remained heavily linked and mutually supporting as the conflict continued over time.

Serendipitously for the Maoists, the last vestige of centralized governmental legitimacy—the Nepalese Royal Family—lost all legitimacy through an apparent regicide, followed by King Gyanendra declaring emergency rule and supplanting the national government. This

Figure 4.2
Feedback Loop Illustrating Causes for COIN Loss in Nepal Maoist Insurgency (with numbered factors)

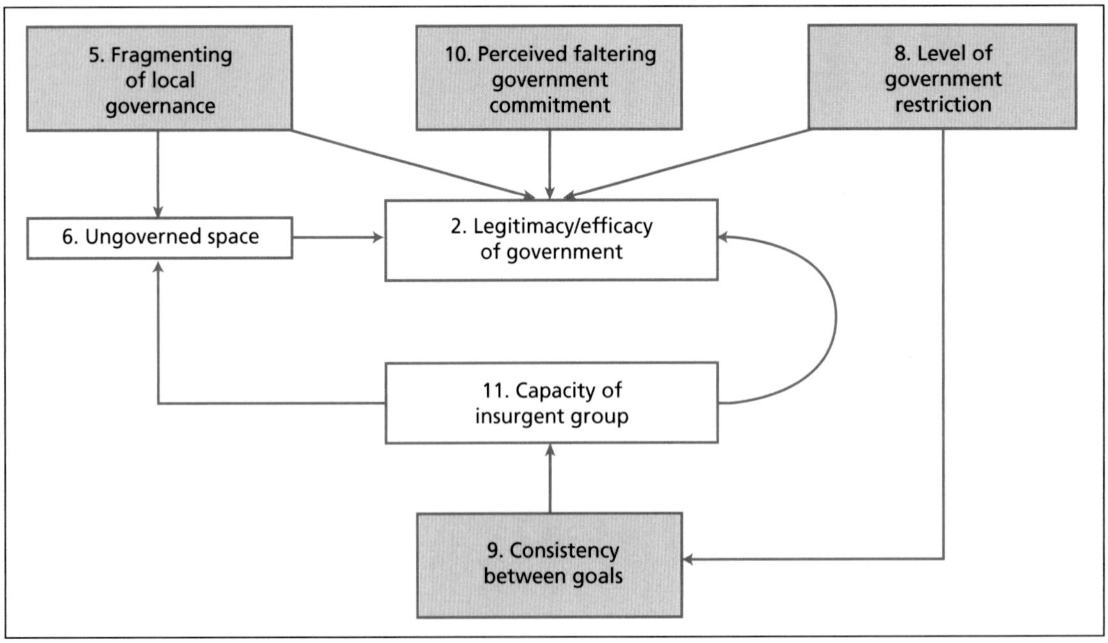

provided a perfect opportunity for the Maoists to stand with an emerging pro-democracy movement against the king and assume both a noble impression and a legitimate role in the new government as it demobilized its military activities. Despite a ten-year history of violence against the state, the Maoists were able to obtain considerable power in the new government and maintain such power to this day.

Concluding Remarks

This chapter analyzed relevant factors in the context of two sponsor-selected insurgencies and demonstrated the interrelationships among the factors. This treatment of two cases provided alternative lenses through which analysts can apply the factors to gain insights into what instigates and perpetuates particular conflict environments.

Interrelationships between factors leading to unstable, conflict-prone environments can create multiple positive feedback loops in which each factor strengthens or exacerbates others successively over time. The Maoist insurgency in Nepal described in this chapter provides such a case in point. In this case, the central government committed multiple missteps—including a combination of an "early head in the sand" attitude and an overly severe but ineffective military and police response—that allowed the initial capacity, public support, and political savvy of the Maoists to increase its yield over time. This led eventually to the fall of the monarchy and the ascendance of the Maoists insurgents to formal political power.

In contrast, when the interrelationships and feedback loops among factors can be disrupted so that the ensuing "web of instability" is weakened rather than strengthened over time, the insurgents may be defeated, and the central government can find it possible to maintain control. For example, in the case of Peru, the central government was able to overcome initial losses to the Shining Path by pursuing its own strategy of economic development in rural areas outside the capital. In addition, a locally based defense and intelligence initiative helped to beat back the Shining Path from these areas. In response, the guerrillas pursued progressively more brutal and repressive tactics, and as such decreased their own legitimacy. Fujimori's government thus severed any nascent links among factors in the region favoring instability (ungoverned space, weak local institutions, etc.), swaying the struggle in their favor and defeating the insurgents.

Applying the factors to particular unstable, conflict-prone environments provides an important step for developing analytic tools that help capture what matters most in such environments. The next chapter extends this analysis by identifying metrics that can help measure each factor and utilizing them in a framework to help decisionmakers set and prioritize levels of analytic and operational effort.

CHAPTER FIVE

Utilizing the Factors for Analysis

This chapter identifies potential metrics that could be used by analysts to detect the presence and assess the strength of each factor in a given context and postulates analytic contexts in which the factors can be employed. Armed with means to measure factors in or across particular countries, analysts could identify local vulnerabilities to the emergence and sustainment of insurgent or terrorist groups and potentially prioritize factors that are of greatest concern. Analysts can use this information to support development of assumptions for wargames and other analyses based on social science research. They can also help inform decisionmakers on the allocation of aid and partner engagement resources to mitigate the negative effects of particular factors.

It is important to note that measuring factors related to environments vulnerable to insurgency and terrorism is exceedingly difficult. In many cases, the metrics we identify may be considered proxies for (rather than direct measurements of) the underlying factors at hand. Also, while for some factors there might be quantitative metrics, in other cases the metric is more qualitative in nature—e.g., "Has there been a history of resistance to central authority or not? How prevalent has this trend been, and what forms has it taken?" Moreover, while our examples in Chapter Three focused on factors during conflict, the Army is also interested in understanding pre-conflict environments, often termed "Phase 0," in which security force assistance to foreign partners is pursued to prevent conflict from occurring in the first place. Analysis of pre-conflict environments is exceedingly challenging. It may be difficult to measure the effects of U.S. security assistance on the factors in such environments. Even if measurements were available and validated, linking the presence or strength of factors to the likelihood or imminence of conflict would be nearly impossible. This is especially true where the United States has limited operational presence and limited abilities to observe or measure the situation "on the ground" (which is especially the case in denied or difficult-to-access areas, such as Syria or Iran).[1]

It is important to recall that the focus of this study was limited to factors that are derived from two particular fields of social science and case examples focused on IW battlefields that have developed primarily over the last dozen years. Factors derived from these fields are important and useful, but only as part of analyses of vulnerable environments that account for the full range of potential exacerbating or mitigating factors in particular political, economic,

---

[1] A more realistic approach would be to assess *vulnerability to* conflict rather than *probability of* conflict. See Sean P. O'Brien, "Anticipating the Good, the Bad, and the Ugly: An Early Warning Approach to Conflict and Instability Analysis," *Journal of Conflict Resolution*, Vol. 46, No. 6, December 2002, pp. 791–811. O'Brien analyzed the relationships between a nation's "macrostructural factors" and the instability a nation has faced during its history to measure the "oily rags" that could lead to conflict rather than predicting the "sparks" that would set it off.

social, geographic, and other contexts.[2] Thus, we offer explication of metrics for assessment of factors, but it is up to the analyst to incorporate them appropriately.

The next section describes potential metrics for each factor. The subsequent section offers some thoughts on ways in which the metrics could be used for analysis.

Metrics for Detecting and Assessing Factors

Table 5.1 provides a summary of metrics for each factor, justification for utility of the metrics, and sources where analysts might find and track them. We identified metrics in some of the anthropological, sociological, and political science sources reviewed for this study and in previous work conducted at RAND to prioritize countries for building partnerships, and established or inferred the metrics' linkage to the factors. In some cases, sources of metrics for some factors, such as history of resistance, rely on anthropological ethnographies of particular populations in conflict zones. These studies may not have been dedicated to establishing history of resistance, but they could be used to glean information for that purpose. For other factors, such as poverty/inequality and repressive government, there are established metrics (e.g., the Human Development Indices and Freedom House reports) that directly measure factor status. We placed emphasis on finding metrics with sources that analysts can easily access and that are automatically updated by owners of the data. This would enable analysts to note changes in observable factors over time (often years rather than days or months) without having to collect input data themselves.

Metrics for Factor 1: External Support

The external support factor has numerous associated direct and surrogate metrics. Direct measurements include the volume and type of financial, logistical, intelligence, and training support provided to the nonstate group. Intelligence reporting may detail external materials that are detected or interdicted as they are trafficked across the host state's borders or as they are collected, stockpiled, and used by the nonstate group; tracking of illicit financing could also support measurement of external support.[3] Less-direct measurements may include the presence of cross-border sanctuaries or rapid shifts in a nonstate group's attack, training, or logistics methodologies. Data sources include the nonstate group's financial ledgers, geospatial intelligence associated with the group's facilities, and databases on illicit and licit arms imports. It may be possible to directly measure external support as it emanates from its foreign source, whether that is a state sponsor or a diaspora community. Human and signals intelligence are likely to be useful sources of information for these metrics. In this case, the challenge to the analyst will be to accumulate this information and then synthesize it to establish a metric that can be used for comparative purposes—i.e., to answer not only whether there is external support, but also how extensive it is in relative terms. The challenge involved in gathering and synthesizing appropriate information applies to several other factors as well.

---

[2]   Ben Connable, *Embracing the Fog of War: Assessment and Metrics in Counterinsurgency*, Santa Monica, Calif: RAND Corporation, MG-1086-DOD, 2012.

[3]   Byman, 2005; and Byman et al., 2001.

Table 5.1
Potential Metrics for Factors

		Metrics	Metric Justification	Data Sources
1.	External support	• Existence of cross-border sanctuaries • Rapid shifts in group capacity • Level/type of external provision of materiel • Foreign source investment in group	• Suggests state or diaspora support/tolerance • Proportion of group capacity, group capacity dependencies	• Regional studies, intelligence reporting (e.g., HUMINT, SIGINT, DocEx, IMINT) • Studies of arms exports, financial ties
2.	Government legitimacy/efficacy	• Level of stability • Level of corruption, public perception of corruption and government legitimacy • Level of basic utilities in key areas	• Indicates overall government effectiveness • Proxy for legitimacy	• Brookings State Weakness Index (141 countries) • State Fragility Index, Polity IV Index
3.	History of resistance	• Frequency of resisted incursions from invaders/outsiders/central government • Level of national and local government struggle to control certain populations	• Surrogate for potential cultural traditions of resistance	• Ethnographies • Liaison reporting • Nonstate conflict database (e.g., Correlates of War) • Press reporting
4.	Poverty/inequality	• Per capita income (by subregion); population below poverty line • Indexes of economic inequality • Existence of "upended" social order	• Income relative to rest of world • Internal income disparities • Indicates disgruntled groups	• CIA Factbook, World Bank • UNDP, Human Development Index • Historiographies, speeches, press reporting
5.	Governance fragmented	• Presence/functioning of local institutions • Quality/type of public services • Infant mortality, life expectancy, crime rates • Individual satisfaction with access	• Availability and local perception of basic services, security, rule of law	• Health, water, crime, other • Polling data
6.	Ungoverned space	• Presence/level of unregulated activities, illegal banking and trafficking • Level of exploitable resources • Terrain difficulty	• Inability of government to monitor/enforce • Attractiveness of area to illicit trade • Government accessibility	• Measures of trafficking, trade routes • Studies of local potential (e.g., oil) • Geography, transportation infrastructure
7.	Multiple armed groups	• Evidence of multiple small conflicts; central government disengagement/irrelevance • Evidence of competing agendas and media operations • Level of violence between competing groups; ethnically targeted terrorism	• Resort to violence against others • Relative tractability, exploitability	• Regional studies, conflict databases • Websites, media operations • Intelligence reporting (e.g., HUMINT, SIGINT), liaison reporting • Press reporting

Table 5.1—continued

		Metrics	Metric Justification	Data Sources
8.	Government repressive	• Level of liberalization • Number of civilian deaths by government • Government use of repressive technologies; level of journalist and dissident imprisonment	• Freedom of expression, press, etc. • Suggests systematic violence	• Freedom House, CPJ • Country Reports on Human Rights • State Fragility Index, Polity IV Index
9.	Goal consistency	• Consistency of group messages • Presence of deep ties/affinities • Success of recruitment campaigns	• Demonstrates narrative focus • Suggests where to look for linkages	• Polling data on local views of groups • Ethnographies • Group media operations, press reporting
10.	Perceived commitment	• Presence of multiple, trusted information outlets • Changing levels of popular support	• Allows varied interpretations of acts • Surrogate for concept of "winner"	• Group, government, international media • Polling data, levels of recruitment
11.	Capacity of groups	• Sophistication of materiel, operations, intelligence, and counterintelligence • Level of finances, number in cadre • Ability to provide alternative services	• Observed ability to adapt behavior • Shows long-term endowment • Demonstrates stewardship	• Studies of individual groups • Intel reporting (e.g., HUMINT, SIGINT), liaison reporting
12.	Social networks	• Prevalence and nature of traditional networks • Level of incorporation of/exploitation by violent nonstate actors • Number of Internet users per 100 people • Volume of traffic on specific sites • Number of mobile telephone subscribers per 100 people	• Characterize traditional networks and insurgent penetration/exploitation • Characterize communication • Communication technology penetration	• Political and demographic histories • Regional studies, ethnographies, detainee reports • World Bank • International Telecommunications Union • Site traffic: Google Trends, Alexa

NOTES: CIA = Central Intelligence Agency, CPJ = Committee to Protect Journalists, DocEx = document exploitation, HUMINT = human intelligence, IMINT = imagery intelligence, SIGINT = signals intelligence, UNDP = United Nations Development Program.

Metrics for Factor 2: Government Legitimacy or Effectiveness

Whether a government is legitimate and effective is a subjective judgment. As a result, reliable metrics associated with this factor are indirect. Measuring legitimacy and effectiveness directly—for example, with public opinion polling—is not feasible in many environments, and even where it is feasible, it may not be reliable. Estimates of a government's level of corruption, and the public's perception of official corruption, can serve as a proxy metric for a government's legitimacy. Effectiveness can be assessed indirectly by gauging a government's level of domestic stability. Stability indexes, including the Brookings State Weakness Index, the State Fragility Index, and the Polity IV Index, offer surrogate measures of a government's effectiveness and its ability to minimize popular discontent. Effectiveness can also be gauged indirectly by examining the population's access to basic services that the government might reasonably be expected to deliver. This may include public health care spending per capita and the availability of basic utilities, such as sanitation and electricity, in targeted areas. The World Bank and UNDP regularly collect this information.

Metrics for Factor 3: History of Resistance

A population's tradition of resistance to invaders and central governments is an important factor in environments prone to insurgency, although it is difficult to measure directly. The frequency with which the population violently confronts invaders and central authority—such as national or provincial-level governance—is a critical surrogate metric. Resistance, however, may often be expressed in subtler and less violent ways. For example, the population may resist paying taxes to a central government or may refrain from facilitating the central government's intelligence collection efforts and policing efforts. Data sources include ethnographies and academic databases that catalogue ethnic conflict, such as the Correlates of War database, which are typically updated regularly. A population's history of resistance can also be estimated with metrics that detail the sophistication and frequency of a government's efforts to forcibly manage the target population through population control procedures and technologies, such as COIN campaigns and propaganda. Some of these data can be acquired through open source press reporting and liaison exchanges with national and provincial security services.

Metrics for Factor 4: Poverty and Inequality

Poverty and inequality metrics are common and are typically reliable. Measures include per capita income by subregion, the percentage of the population below the poverty line, estimates of internal income disparities, and economic inequality relative to neighboring countries and the rest of the world. The World Bank, the World Health Organization, the UNDP's Human Development Index, and the CIA's World Factbook are good sources of information. The existence of an "upended" social order is a critical, although potentially elusive, inequality metric. Evidence of rapid or dramatic shifts in a particular social group's economic or political status could help to forecast the emergence of disgruntled groups. A very stark example of this mentioned in Chapter Three is related to the development of the insurgency in Iraq during Operation Iraqi Freedom, where the sudden removal by force of the Ba'athists from power created the conditions for the Sunni uprising. Sources of data for this variable might include historiographies, press reporting, and political speeches. The availability of these data is likely to vary widely by region and individual country.

Metrics for Factor 5: Fragmented Governance

A government's ability to consistently provide public services, from health and sanitation to judicial services and law enforcement, is an important factor in determining an environment's susceptibility to violent extremist groups. The presence and functionality of local institutions is a key metric. This can be assessed directly by gauging the quality and type of public services available to a population in particular subregions, such as public health care spending, the level of sanitation services, and electricity access per capita. The functionality of local institutions may also be estimated indirectly from a population's rate of infant mortality, deaths from communicable diseases, electricity usage, murder, and crime. The World Bank and UNDP regularly collect this type of information. A population's satisfaction with its access to public services is also a useful metric. This may be assessed with public opinion polling data, although these data are typically scarce in remote regions and may be unreliable. In regions with ongoing large-scale stability operations (such as Afghanistan), U.S. military and civilian authorities systematically track the capabilities and service provision capacities of local governments.

Metrics for Factor 6: Ungoverned Space

Ungoverned territories develop for numerous reasons, but many result from a combination of the territory's inaccessibility and the central government's relative weakness. Not all inaccessible regions with challenging terrain will be ungovernable, but states with limited resources typically have trouble maintaining control or influence in such areas. Additionally, ungoverned space will be of interest especially if a violent extremist group is in the process of exploiting it or is planning to do so. Powerful nonstate authorities are particularly likely to emerge and thrive in areas where exploitable resources and ungoverned space are co-located. Indicators of ungoverned space include the absence of official governing authorities and law enforcement elements; the presence of powerful governing alternatives to central authority; and the presence of exploitable resources or officially unregulated and illicit financial, logistical, and policing activities in or near population centers.[4] Additional related metrics include the presence of trafficking and illicit trade routes in combination with difficult terrain or inaccessible territories where insurgents or their sympathizers are concentrated. These metrics will provide insight into the importance of an ungoverned territory and the central or provincial government's ability to surge military personnel and equipment into the territory.

Metrics for Factor 7: Multiple Armed Groups

Metrics related to armed groups span two main categories: the presence of multiple armed groups and the level and sustainability of violence associated with their confrontations. Measurements related to their presence include evidence of multiple small conflicts; terrorist attacks against specific ethnic, tribal, or religious subgroups; and localized conflicts in which the central government is a secondary, or irrelevant, player.[5] Data sources include regional studies, conflict databases, and press reporting. Measurements related to the level and sustainability of violence associated with armed group conflict include the volume of weapons trafficking into a conflict area, the number of deaths per year resulting from the conflict, the competing groups' commitments to their violent agendas, and evidence of outside support from state and nonstate elements. This type of information will most likely be acquired through clandestine intelligence and liaison reporting but may be available in press reporting, depending on the country. Data sources associated with armed group metrics will typically be updated periodically, depending on the region, the conflict, and the sophistication and engagement of the associated liaison services.

Metrics for Factor 8: Government Repression

The repressiveness of a government can be measured directly and indirectly. Direct measurements include the level and type of violence used to suppress a population, the government's use of repressive intelligence and counterintelligence tools against its population—such as physical surveillance platforms, informants, and technical eavesdropping measures—and the

---

4   Rabasa et al., 2007.

5   Rabasa et al., 2007.

intensity of government efforts to arrest and imprison political dissidents, human rights workers, and journalists. Clandestine reporting, press reporting, and periodic country reports published by such groups as Human Rights Watch, the Committee to Protect Journalists, and Freedom House are generally good data sources for these metrics. Less-direct measurements include broad assessments of a government's level of liberalization and civilian deaths caused by the government, which may implicate the government in the application of deadly, repressive force. The State Fragility Index and the Polity IV Index are useful, annually updated sources of information on levels of repressiveness and liberalization by country.

Metrics for Factor 9: Insurgent Group and Population Goal Consistency

The level of consistency between the insurgent group's goals and those of the target population is a critical factor in an unstable environment. Goal consistency is an inherently subjective outcome—it is typically estimated, therefore, with surrogate metrics and is analytically challenging to measure for comparative purposes. Metrics include the level of agreement between insurgent messaging and propaganda and the population's political, social, and economic objectives; the presence of deep ties between the insurgent group and the population; and the success of insurgent recruitment operations targeted at the population. These measures will help to determine whether the insurgent group has developed a cleverly tailored narrative to leverage popular grievances. Additionally, the measures may help to identify support linkages between the insurgent group and key subsegments of the population. Goal consistency can be measured more directly, in certain circumstances, by gauging public opinion, although, as previously mentioned, clandestine polling is challenging and occasionally unreliable. Sources of information for goal consistency metrics include press reporting, insurgent media outputs, ethnographic studies, and liaison reporting. In some cases, public polling may provide some insight into public attitudes toward insurgent or terrorist groups.

Metrics for Factor 10: Perceived Government Commitment

Subjective perception of a government's commitment to a COIN campaign is among the most challenging factors to estimate and analyze. Perceptions may differ between the target population and the insurgent group and may also shift rapidly. Where reliable polling data cannot be acquired, useful proxy metrics include the presence of "trusted" media reporting on the government's resolve, the presence of multiple media and other information outlets to which the population and insurgent group have access, shifts in the level of popular support for an insurgent group and its activities, and shifts in recruitment levels. Data sources for insurgent group perception include clandestine human and signals intelligence targeting key group leaders and opinionmakers. Data sources for the population's perceptions include polling, local and international press reporting, and intelligence reporting on popular support for the group. These information sources may be updated regularly, depending on the region and conflict. Media content analysis of the insurgent or nonstate actor's public statements, press releases, and propaganda by those with good working knowledge of the local population's value system and cultural proclivities could also prove useful for measuring this factor. Increasingly, population support for (or opposition to) local nonstate actors might be expressed in blogs or social networking posts, although this is contingent on monitoring, repression, and reprisals for these expressions of public opinion.

Metrics for Factor 11: Capacity of Armed Group

Metrics associated with an armed group's capacity can be divided into five main categories of capability: leadership, warfighting, population support, logistics and sustainment, and counterintelligence. The quality of leadership is difficult to measure but may be indirectly assessed by evaluating relative group cohesiveness, resilience and structure of chain of command, and adaptability of the group to changes in circumstances and adversary strategy. Metrics related to warfighting include the quantity and sophistication of the group's operations, weapons, and personnel. Population support metrics include measurements of the sophistication of the group's media operations and its ability to deliver public services, as well as public polling data or other more direct evidence (e.g., public financing) of support. Logistics and sustainment metrics include the sophistication of the group's financial and human capital operations, such as its recruitment operations and its management of connections to external sponsors.[6] Finally, metrics associated with counterintelligence include the sophistication of the group's human and signals intelligence and counterespionage operations. Data for many of these metrics can be acquired through clandestine intelligence and liaison reporting, and a few can be gauged through press reporting and individual studies of armed groups.

Metrics for Factor 12: Social Networks

Measuring the strength of social networks and their penetration by insurgent or terrorist groups is by no means straightforward. Additionally, it is important to understand modes of network communication, which can occur in either virtual or traditional, "direct contact" mediums. Direct contact (traditional) social networking is often informal and, therefore, quite difficult to monitor and track. A qualitative assessment of the vitality of a population's traditional networks may serve as a practical surrogate metric. Ethnographies, regional studies, demographic assessments, local security service reporting, and detainee information will likely facilitate this analysis by adding complementary data. Virtual networking can be measured directly in some environments by observing the volume of relevant traffic on target websites, message boards, and chat forums. A host of "social networking capacity" metrics offer a less direct method for gauging virtual interaction volume. These variables include the proportion of Internet users and mobile telephone subscribers in a target population and whether the population has access to and a social or cultural propensity to use virtual networking platforms. Such data sources as the International Telecommunications Union and the World Bank are regularly updated.

Applying the Factors in Analysis

The metrics offered in Table 5.1 can be viewed in two analytic contexts. First, they can help determine the prevailing conditions in a region of interest or study. These include

- *detecting the presence of a factor,* whereby the analyst defines a minimum threshold (in some cases, anything above zero) beyond which the factor should be considered relevant to an environment
- *measuring the strength of a factor* in absolute terms to allow tracking of changes
- *assessing the salience of a factor* relative to other factors in an environment

---

[6]   Weinstein, 2006.

- *measuring the relationships among multiple factors* and their cumulative effect on an environment.

The level of difficulty and complexity increases substantially as one moves from the top of the list to the bottom of the list. Detecting the presence of a factor may be as simple as answering a yes/no question—for example, whether or not an insurgent group is active in a region or whether there has been a history of tribal resistance to central authority. Measuring the strength or prevalence of a factor may be somewhat more complex. Putting an absolute measure on "government fragmentation," for instance, is not straightforward, but it may be made more meaningful through comparisons with other regions or countries (which could result in the creation of a rating or ranking scheme). Assessing how important a factor might be relative to other factors in a specific environment is made even more challenging by the difficulty in directly linking it to outcomes. For example, it is problematic to deterministically link levels of poverty to popular support for and success of an insurgency or government in a specific situation. In fact, when formal analyses of the link between poverty and insurgency are made (controlling for other factors), this relationship often comes into question.[7] Finally, evaluating interdependencies among several factors and assessing their cumulative effects presents the greatest challenge of all. Exhaustive studies of insurgencies often disagree on such assessments even after the fact; evaluation during a conflict, much less before one has arisen, raises significantly greater uncertainty. Whether such assessments are qualitative or quantitative, evidence can often be interpreted in a wide variety of ways, leading analysts to come to very different conclusions even when using similar data sets and sources.

Second, analysts can use the metrics to assess actual or expected effects on factors of mitigating actions by U.S. or partner forces, exacerbating actions by nonstate adversaries and their supporters, and other emerging circumstances (such as natural disasters). *Actual effects* would be those observed over time after an action or set of actions has been taken to mitigate or strengthen a factor. Alternatively, *expected effects* refer to relationships between cause and effect that might be derived from similar historical cases and used in "what-if" analysis. For example, one might use leadership-related measures of group capacity to observe actual effects of Guzman's capture on the capacity of the Shining Path and later apply lessons of the group's decapitation to analysis of potential counter-leadership actions in other similar insurgencies and environments.

Using the Factors to Prioritize Level of Effort

As mentioned previously, there is great interest in DoD in understanding the susceptibility of regions or nations to the rise of unstable, conflict-prone environments and taking actions (or helping partner nations take actions) to prevent insurgency, terrorism, and other violence and instability before they reach levels that might necessitate deployment of U.S. combat forces. Actions that the U.S. military could take in Phase 0 include assisting populations in humanitarian need, building and supporting infrastructure in areas lacking basic services, and training and advising partner nation forces to help provide services and security in ways that respect human rights.

---

[7]   Alan B. Krueger and Jitka Maleckova, "Education, Poverty and Terrorism: Is There a Causal Connection?" *Journal of Economic Perspectives*, Vol. 17, No. 4, Fall 2003, pp. 119–144.

One question that joint and service decisionmakers and planners must address is how to allocate resources globally across areas that could give rise to such environments. For instance, where should U.S. security assistance be applied to prevent or minimize insurgency, terrorism, and other forms of violence and instability in potential zones of conflict where U.S. interests are at stake? How should assistance be tailored to address the most-salient factors present in these zones? A scheme for assessing vulnerability of states and regions to instabilities and tracking trends in them would benefit decisions on where to conduct Phase 0 activities and in what form, and the factors could provide a foundation for such a scheme.

An assessment scheme would evaluate potential conflict zones around the world, most easily by country, with the countries having the greatest potential for conflict or those with the most desperate needs being given greater emphasis in analytic efforts designed to shape Phase 0 assistance. It would begin with measurement of the factors and derivation of absolute values for each; these could be from sources that measure value, as well as those that compare values across countries. Table 5.2 provides an example of an assessment scheme.

Because the raw metrics are likely to reflect differing scales, the analyst might create an index that standardizes the metrics to one scale—e.g., between 0 and 1. Consider two countries, Country I and Country II, and Factors Q, R, and S. Factors Q and R each have two metrics that measure factor presence and strength, while Factor S has a single metric. Each of the metrics is expressed on a different scale, such as by rank (e.g., global stability ranking), qualitative level of presence (e.g., strong or weak history of resistance), or percentage of population (e.g., of minority ethnic background). Indexing the varied raw scores provides indexed metric scores between 0 and 1 (e.g., Country I ranks 132nd out of 192 countries in terms of stability, yielding 132/192 = 0.69).

This example assumes that when there are multiple metrics for a given factor, these metrics are given equal importance (i.e., they are weighted evenly). In some cases, the analyst may

Table 5.2
Sample Assessment Scheme Based on Factors

Country	Factor	Metric	Raw Metric Score	Indexed Metric Score	Current	Trend
Country I	Factor Q	Metric a (rank)	132	0.69		–
		Metric b (level)	Strong	0.75		–
	Factor R	Metric c (score)	3.7	0.65		–
		Metric d ($/capita)	$765	0.83		/
	Factor S	Metric e (%)	39%	0.39		/
Country II	Factor Q	Metric a (rank)	84	0.44		+
		Metric b (level)	Weak	0.25		/
	Factor R	Metric c (score)	1.6	0.22		+
		Metric d ($/capita)	$2,450	0.48		–
	Factor S	Metric e (%)	10%	0.10		/

NOTES: Green = 0–0.33, yellow = 0.34–0.67, red = 0.68–1.0. Positive trend: +, negative trend: –, no change: /.

give greater importance or validity to some metrics over others, and thereby give them different weights between 0 and 1. For instance, if weighting two metrics evenly, one would multiply each indexed value by 0.5; alternatively, one metric twice as important as another in measuring a factor would be multiplied by 0.67, and the other by 0.33. The two metrics would then be added together to get a raw factor score. Analytic discussions over weightings of metrics, and even the factors themselves, are important parts of the process leading to resource allocation recommendations. But weightings must be transparent to—and ultimately even set by—the decisionmaker, lest analysts inadvertently skew the results of their assessments.

The metric scores can then be presented as a stoplight assessment, for example, with metric scores of 0–0.33 shaded green, 0.34–0.67 shaded yellow, and 0.68–1.0 shaded red. Thus, given that Country A ranks relatively low for stability, its indexed 0.69 measure would earn it a red shading. For factors that are measured mainly in qualitative terms, the analyst would need to translate qualitative assessments into quantitative measures—e.g., defining a history of resistance to central government as "strong," "moderate," or "weak" and associating a quantity with each, such as 1.0 (red), 0.67 (yellow), and 0.33 (green), respectively. In addition, the analyst might assess the prevailing trends for each metric and associated factor. In other words, one could note that the metrics of a factor are getting worse ("–"), getting better ("+"), or unchanging over time ("/")—combined with a stoplight color—to provide a sense of a factor's potential status without the intervention of external changes or influences. Alternatively, more detailed analysis of a factor and its metric(s) in specific situations might yield insights about trends that are changing.

This assessment scheme could then be used to narrow the grouping of nations that may require focus for Phase 0 assistance and supporting analysis. Analysts might simply sum the indexed metric scores and preferentially focus on the countries with the highest overall scores. In the examples provided in Table 5.2 (and assuming that there are only three factors and five metrics), Country I would yield an overall score of 3.31 (0.69 + 0.75 + 0.65 + 0.83 + 0.39), and Country II a score of 1.49 (0.44 + 0.25 + 0.22 + 0.48 + 0.10), indicating that the factors potentially creating conditions in which insurgency or terrorism might arise are more prevalent in Country I than in Country II. Analysts could then group nations like Country I (e.g., countries with an overall score greater than, say, 3.0) to provide insight on where to allocate analytic resources and, potentially, security assistance resources.

More detailed evaluation of factors in countries with high overall scores, as well as analysis of trends in factors and the interrelationships among them, would need to follow this assessment scheme to identify appropriate means of addressing them. Importantly, this scheme does not weight factors (or, more accurately, it weights them evenly), yet such weighting would be an important part of any analysis or resource allocation decision. Weighting could be accomplished by decisionmakers informed by their own experience and by analysis of salient factors in specific contexts. Analysts could provide insight to decisionmakers by demonstrating how varying the weightings could affect prioritization and recommendations for how resources could best be allocated.

Concluding Remarks

This chapter presented a set of metrics by which analysts of unstable environments could detect the presence and evaluate the salience of sociologically and anthropologically based factors that help create and sustain those environments. Inasmuch as metrics are quantitative, efforts are made to identify sources of data that are tracked and regularly updated by established institutions and can be easily accessed by analysts. In addition, the chapter proposed a construct for assessing countries and regions based on the presence of factors that may make indigenous populations and governments more vulnerable to the emergence of environments in which violent extremist groups could thrive.

While a number of the metrics are quantitative, in many cases they serve more as proxies or surrogates for the associated factor than as direct measurements. Other metrics are qualitative in nature but can still serve as meaningful ways of assessing a factor or comparing the prevalence of a factor in one conflict to its presence in other conflicts. In some cases, measurement of factors is limited to historiographies and other studies that do not offer a clear-cut "metric" per se, but these studies can provide insights that the analyst must translate into inputs relevant to analytic constructs or models. In other cases, metrics may rely on perishable polling data whose availability is inconsistent. These challenges in measuring factors at times will render the utility of individual metrics less than satisfactory. It is hoped that by offering multiple metrics for each factor, some of these challenges can be somewhat mitigated.

CHAPTER SIX

Conclusion

This study provided a review of sources of understanding about what instigates and perpetuates unstable environments susceptible to insurgency and terrorism—in which IW may be engaged—from the fields of sociology, cultural anthropology, political science, and related fields of social science. The study identified and analyzed factors, assessed levels of consensus among experts about their salience in those environments, and provided examples in which the factors can be applied. It also proposed metrics for each factor that could support analyses of environments and assessment of countries and regions based on the relative strength of the factors. These research results should help members of the defense analytic community assess what matters in these environments to inform decisionmakers on allocation of analytic resources and, ultimately, resources associated with security assistance and operational efforts.

Key Findings

The following findings emerged from our research:

- While U.S. military doctrine espouses a number of root causes and perpetuators of environments in which IW is engaged, it does not offer critical analysis of the concepts. A review of U.S. Army and joint doctrine indicates that the delineation of causes and trends is relatively consistent across doctrinal publications. However, military doctrine does not question the utility of the concepts in specific circumstances, nor does it acknowledge that there could be uncertainty among social scientists about the salience of these concepts across disparate zones of potential conflict.
- Sociology, anthropology, and related fields offer insights into instigators and perpetuators of environments vulnerable to insurgencies and terrorism. Application of such constructs as social network theory (sociology) and cultures of violence (anthropology) to the study of these environments sheds light on the interplay between individuals' personal inclinations, beliefs, or position in a society and the political, economic, and organizational structures in which they are situated. Other theories from political science and microeconomics can augment the sociological and anthropological ones.
- Twelve underlying factors relevant to unstable environments prone to violent extremism can be discerned from the fields of sociology, anthropology, and related fields. The research team validated and vetted these factors through a combination of a survey of peer-reviewed literature, comparison with detailed COIN case studies, and focused discussions with social scientists.

- Agreement in the literature and among experts regarding the salience of these factors generally was high. Disagreement tended to center on the degree to which the factors are universally applicable and the relative importance of certain subfactors. In general, the anthropological literature did not establish consensus but pointed out case-by-case differences in the relevance of various factors we identified.
- Factors are linked to one another through complex, mutually dependent interrelationships. There are multiple feedback loops in which each factor strengthens or exacerbates others over time in a given conflict. Where these interrelationships can be disrupted, individual factors can be weakened as sources of instability or sustainment of violence.
- Qualitative and quantitative metrics can be developed that enable assessment and tracking of factors. Qualitative metrics may provide insights to the analyst but require translation into inputs relevant to analytic constructs or models. Quantitative metrics can be used to directly measure the prevalence of a factor in an environment, but this is rare, given the nature of these environments. More often, they serve as surrogates for associated factors. There are a number of relevant metrics in the public domain that are updated annually and can be easily accessed for analysis.
- Metrics can be used in a scheme for assessing and prioritizing countries and regions based on the presence of factors that could give rise to unstable environments. Such a scheme could help U.S. planners and analysts focus level of effort and identify priorities for resource allocation globally across regions that are susceptible to violence and instability.

Recommendations

We recommend that the U.S. Army analytic community take the following actions:

- **Incorporate factors and associated metrics into IW-related analytic games and models.** Supplement existing tools with components that enable consideration of the relative strength of factors in particular scenarios and encourage concepts for mitigating negative effects on the fight.
- **Evaluate levels of potential instability and extremist violence using the assessment scheme outlined in this report.** Analysts can track trends in factor prevalence in particular countries or regions to alert decisionmakers to growing areas of instability or to follow the consequences of U.S. or local government action.
- **Conduct research to probe and map overlays and interrelationships among factors in specific cases.** Such research would indicate where overlays exist and how factors interact with each other. Research on Iraq and Afghanistan, two environments with which U.S. analysts are intimately familiar and where understanding is relatively fresh, should be considered.
- **Develop a prioritization approach based on the factors and assessment scheme that helps indicate where best to allocate analytic and security assistance resources.** Analysts may use the factors and associated metrics not only to track sources of instability or conflict in states and regions but also to prioritize allocation of resources. This would require development of a transparent approach that weights alternative metrics for each factor, and even the factors themselves.

Concluding Remarks

Analysts of IW and unstable environments susceptible to extremist violence can use the factors derived from social science research to explore means of mitigating their effects during conflict and to head off conflict before it occurs. More detailed analysis is needed to understand how actions by U.S. and partner forces affect the presence and strength of factors in specific conflict zones. It is hoped that the research contained in this report makes an important contribution to the growing body of work in the social sciences dedicated to understanding the sources of environments in which IW may need to be considered.

Factors from Joint and Army Doctrine

U.S. doctrine sheds some light on factors believed to give rise to instabilities associated with insurgency and terrorism. There are significant commonalities among U.S. doctrinal publications on the indicators and root causes of environments vulnerable to the rise of violent extremist groups and IW. Some of the doctrinal literature examines underlying components of the operational environment that may elicit irregular conflicts. U.S. Army Field Manual 3-0 identifies trends in "persistent conflicts," which it defines as "a protracted confrontation among state, non-state, and individual actors that are increasingly willing to use violence to achieve their political and ideological ends."[1] It lists these trends as follows:

- technology
- demographic changes
- urbanization
- demand for finite resources
- climate change and natural disasters
- weapons of mass destruction (WMD) proliferation and effects
- failed or failing states
- globalization.

The 2010 Department of Defense Joint Operating Concept (JOC) for Irregular Warfare offers many of the same trends and components. It generalizes the trends as follows:

> Economic, demographic, resource, climate, and other trends will engender competition locally, regionally, and globally. Global integration, intense nationalism, and religious movements will likely exacerbate the tensions created by each of these trends. Frequent conflicts will erupt among sub-state ethnic, tribal, religious, and political groups. State fragmentation, transnational crime, the globalized movement of capital, competition for resources, and migration and urbanization will all contribute to the likelihood of conflict in this complex and fluid environment.[2]

The JOC offers ungoverned spaces as a particularly concerning byproduct of failed and failing states that can lead to IW. The JOC notes that

---

[1] Headquarters, Department of the Army, *Field Manual 3-0: Operations*, February 2008, p. 15.

[2] DoD, 2010b, pp. 11–12.

of particular concern are failed and failing states, which could lead to more 'ungoverned spaces,' which become safe havens for terrorists, criminals, and groups engaged in other illicit activities. These 'spaces' could be rural, urban, maritime, air, or 'virtual.'[3]

Taking a more granular approach than assessment of environmental components, U.S. Army *Field Manual 3-05.202: Special Forces Foreign Internal Defense Operations* examines possible triggers, referred to as *initiating events*, that would set an insurgent movement into action. These triggers include events that gain symbolic significance (such as an individual's heroic act of defiance) or that force action (such as foreign invasion), emergence of a charismatic leader, and the perception of a tactical or strategic advance by a revolutionary elite.[4]

Doctrinal publications offer insights into the factors that sustain IW once it has already been set into action. For example, U.S. Army Field Manual (FM) 3-24, *Counterinsurgency*, mentions the role of transnational criminal activities in supporting and sustaining IW and the law enforcement activities required to counter them.[5] Pointing to the defeat of the Abu Sayyaf Group and Jemaah Islamiyah in the Philippines in 2008, the Center for Army Lessons Learned (CALL), in *Newsletter 11-34: Irregular Warfare, A SOF* [Special Operations Forces] *Perspective*, describes freedom of movement and the access to basic necessities as requirements for sustaining irregular warfighters.[6] Offering another example, CALL mentions the critical importance of popular support for successful efforts to end a foreign occupation or topple a hostile government. FM 3-05.202 adds that "the insurgents need the active support of a majority of the politically active people and the passive acquiescence of the majority."[7]

Within the theme of organizational leadership, certain publications suggest that the sustainment of IW is contingent not just on effective leadership within the nonstate organization, but also on its ability to emulate, and ultimately replace, the state itself. FM 3-0 suggests the following:

> Extremist organizations adopt state-like qualities using the media, technology, and their position within a state's political, military and social infrastructures to their advantage. Their operations grow more sophisticated, combining conventional, unconventional, irregular, and criminal tactics. They focus on creating conditions of instability, seek to alienate legitimate forces from the population, and employ global networks to expand local operations.[8]

Similarly, FM 3-05.202 contends the following:

> Leaders of the insurgency must make their cause known to the people and gain popular support. Their key tasks are to break the ties between the people and the government and

---

[3] DoD, 2010b, p. 12.

[4] Headquarters, Department of the Army, *Field Manual 3-05.202: Special Forces Foreign Internal Defense Operations*, February 2007, Section A-7, p. 49.

[5] Headquarters, Department of the Army, *FM 3-24: Counterinsurgency*, December 2006, pp. 21–23.

[6] CALL, 2011, p. 73.

[7] Headquarters, Department of the Army, 2007, Section A-2, p. 44.

[8] Headquarters, Department of the Army, 2008, p. 18.

to establish the credibility of their movement. They must replace the legitimacy of the government with that of their own.[9]

Thus, U.S. military doctrine does offer views on the causes and perpetuators of environments that DoD associates with IW. However, it does not provide critical analysis of concepts, nor does it acknowledge some uncertainty among social scientists about the salience of these concepts across disparate zones of potential conflict.

---

[9] Headquarters, Department of the Army, 2007, Section A-4, p. 45.

Factor Matrix

Table B.1
Instigators/Perpetuators of Unstable, Conflict-Prone Environments ("Factor Matrix")

Factor Number	Factor	Key Aspects	Brief Description	Mitigating/ Exacerbating Variables	Metrics and Data Sources	Analytic Questions	Level of Consensus About Salience of Factor	Conflict Examples
1	External support for violent, nonstate groups	Outside support can originate from state or nonstate entities and typically includes the provision of weapons, money, intelligence, training, safe haven, diplomatic support, ideological support, and/ or logistical assistance.	External state or nonstate entities connected to (and promoting the growth of) violent groups inside the host country	Extent and type of external support	Evidence of external financial, logistical, or materiel aid in violent, nonstate actor weapons, equipment, or records. Evidence of external financial aid in international financial transactions.	Are violent, nonstate groups receiving support from an external actor? If so, what kind of support is the external actor providing (financial, logistical, intelligence, training)?	There is a relatively high degree of consensus in the literature for this factor, particularly among political scientists, and closely related phenomena studied by sociologists and anthropologists.	Iran's support for Hizbollah, Pakistan's support for Lashkar-e-Tayyiba, the Somali diaspora's support for al-Shabbab, Libya's support for the Irish Republican Army, Liberia's support for the Revolutionary United Front in Sierra Leone, and Greece's support for the Kurdistan Workers' Party
			Diaspora connected to and providing financial and/or logistical support to violent groups	Intentions of the external actor providing support	Evidence of external training or ideological reorientation in violent, nonstate actor behavior; tactics, techniques, and procedures (TTPs); or public statements.	What are the intentions of the external actor providing support?		
			Government and nongovernment elements in neighboring country allow violent groups to establish cross-border sanctuaries.	Existence of cross-border sanctuaries	Evidence of violent, nonstate actor movement from an external safe haven to an area of operations	Where and how large are the group's sanctuaries or controlled territory?		

Table B.1—continued

Factor Number	Factor	Key Aspects	Brief Description	Mitigating/ Exacerbating Variables	Metrics and Data Sources	Analytic Questions	Level of Consensus About Salience of Factor	Conflict Examples
2	Government considered illegitimate or ineffective by the population	Weak and failed states are at great risk of becoming havens for transnational terrorist and guerrilla groups partially because of critical capacity gaps, as well as perceptions of a rise to power through means not accepted by the majority of the populace.	Government is perceived to be unrepresentative by the population and perceived to be failing to provide basic services.	Location and extent of popular discontent

Extent of violent opposition responses

Government security service effectiveness

Role of violent, nonstate groups in perpetuating grievances | Violent, nonstate groups fill the "provision of services" void and play on local grievances to enhance their popular appeal.

Polling of population shows low confidence in public officials and their ability to provide adequate governance

High levels of official corruption | What segments of the population consider the government illegitimate? How influential or powerful are each of these segments?

How has the population or key elements of the population been successful in violently opposing the host government?

What can the government be expected to accomplish with its security services?

Where have these groups made the greatest headway in shaping popular perceptions? In recruiting and fundraising? In mobilizing fighters? | There is very high (almost universal) agreement that this factor is salient in the production and maintenance of unstable, conflict-prone environments over time. | Yemen (AQAP, 2011), Somalia (Warlords, 1993–2011), Palestinian Liberation Organization (1970s–1980s), Hizbollah in Lebanon, Rwandan Hutu Interahamwe, Nicaraguan Contras |

Table B.1—continued

Factor Number	Factor	Key Aspects	Brief Description	Mitigating/ Exacerbating Variables	Metrics and Data Sources	Analytic Questions	Level of Consensus About Salience of Factor	Conflict Examples
3	Tribal or ethnic indigenous populations with history of resisting state rule and/or cultures that encourage or justify violent behavior	This factor includes two different cultural patterns: (1) a proclivity toward intensely localized social organization and government (i.e., ignoring or resisting central governance) and (2) the normalization, justification, and sometimes glorification of violence as a proper means of resolving disputes.	Host country perforated with tribal systems that resist centralized governance, especially coupled with local cultures/ subcultures of violence	Extent and type of influence of local social systems and groups that resist centralized control

Existence of forbidding terrain and/ or licit or illicit local subsistence modes that are hard to track, monitor, or tax. Capacity of the state to extend monitoring, infrastructure, and control to remote locations and formerly untracked forms of livelihood or trade.

Substantive connections between these groups and violent external actors. | Influential social groups currently successfully resisting state rule by violent means.

The presence of social groups with social norms that promote or justify violent behavior. Can include media used to desensitize individuals or glorify violent actions.

State has given up fighting in certain areas due to heavy resistance from tribes. | Where are various groups located, and what is the extent of their influence over the local population and local policies?

What are the underlying reasons for a culture or set of practices designed to resist centralized rule?

What are the various local cultures of violence, and how are these cultural norms promoted and maintained? | There is strong disagreement in the literature regarding this factor. This is due to the fact that there is significant debate regarding the degree to which these cultural patterns are inherently bound to specific groups or are due to the influence of social context. | Chechnya, Sandinistas in El Salvador, Palestinian Occupied Territories (second Intifada), Iraq during OIF, Afghanistan (Taliban 2001), Upland Southeast Asia, modern Mexico |

Table B.1—continued

Factor Number	Factor	Key Aspects	Brief Description	Mitigating/ Exacerbating Variables	Metrics and Data Sources	Analytic Questions	Level of Consensus About Salience of Factor	Conflict Examples
3 (cont.)						Do these groups support or provide sanctuary (or even personnel/ labor) to violent or terrorist groups? If so, what is the appeal of these groups to the local population (ethnic or religious identity, provision of protection, support coerced, etc.)?		

Table B.1—continued

Factor Number	Factor	Key Aspects	Brief Description	Mitigating/ Exacerbating Variables	Metrics and Data Sources	Analytic Questions	Level of Consensus About Salience of Factor	Conflict Examples
4	Absolute poverty or relative inequality, especially the presence of one or more groups that have recently lost status or power and consider themselves to have a rightfully dominant position in the local hierarchy (a "claim to the throne")	There are several pathways by which scholars have suggested that this factor contributes to instability. The first is that poor or destitute individuals might be more vulnerable to real or promised financial incentives from nonstate actors. A second line of thought is whether certain subgroups in a population perceive the distribution of wealth or power to be unjust.	Absolute poverty, status inequities, and social disruption, especially combined with a mismatch between the expectations and social/economic realities of specific groups within the population	Ability for COIN elements to create local employment opportunities and grow local economy Ability and willingness of government to recognize and formally incorporate disenfranchised, disenchanted, or frustrated groups Degree to which cultural belief systems justify (or decry) the inequitable distribution of wealth, privilege, and power	Local subsistence patterns and vulnerabilities, including seasonal availability of food, fuel, and other essential items Indices of economic inequality, such as the Gini coefficient Historical documents, modern speeches, and other media referring to an "old" or "proper" social order in which currently disempowered groups held more power and influence	Is the local population living below subsistence levels and vulnerable to incentives from insurgent groups for sporadic combat support, intelligence, or other labor? Has the social hierarchy or relative status of groups recently been "shaken up" through intervention from outside entities, internal revolutions, or other events? Are there groups that have recently lost power or status and have a strong leader or movement mobilizing this group to action?	There is moderate agreement in the literature regarding the role of relative deprivation and perceived injustices of inequality in causing instability and leading to violent environments. The link between poverty alone and terrorist recruits, in particular, has come into question.	Ba'athists in Iraq, Rwandan genocide, Palestinian Occupied Territories, multiple Latin American conflicts

Table B.1—continued

Factor Number	Factor	Key Aspects	Brief Description	Mitigating/ Exacerbating Variables	Metrics and Data Sources	Analytic Questions	Level of Consensus About Salience of Factor	Conflict Examples
5	Local governance fragmented, weak, or vulnerable to replacement or co-option from insurgent replacement institutions	In some unstable environments, local systems for the provision of schooling, health care, dispute resolution, group decisionmaking, or other services are either very rudimentary or insufficient, have recently broken down, or can be pushed aside through coercion or intimidation by nonstate actors. One way for insurgent groups to take and hold ground is to fill this civil governance gap by providing schooling (even if radicalized and ideological), health care, rule of law, or other services.	Lack of ability of local authorities to: • provide basic services (health, water, sanitary, veterinary, etc.) • uphold rule of law (systems of detainment, investigation, prosecution) • promote economic prosperity and growth • resolve land and property disputes/protect the rights of property owners	Ability for COIN elements to provide stopgap governance and rule of law capabilities and (when possible) to connect these to state governance

Degree to which the local population expects the provision of certain types of social services

Absolute need (for basic survival) of the population | Presence and functioning of local institutions

Presence of shadow governance and justice systems

State of local economy and economic mobility

Polling data on individual satisfaction with access to services, security, etc. | What is the state of local governance and rule of law?

How well-functioning, accessible, and integrated are local systems for providing basic services? Are they available to all? Are they predictable and dependable? Are they connected with central governance?

Are insurgents targeting weaknesses or gaps in these institutions? | There is strong agreement in the literature about the salience of this factor for unstable environments that perpetuate violence. | Al Qaeda in Pakistan, Taliban in Afghanistan, Hamas in the Gaza Strip, Hizbollah in Lebanon |

Table B.1—continued

Factor Number	Factor	Key Aspects	Brief Description	Mitigating/ Exacerbating Variables	Metrics and Data Sources	Analytic Questions	Level of Consensus About Salience of Factor	Conflict Examples
6	Ungoverned space	Ungoverned territory, characterized by a lack of state penetration, physical infrastructure, monopoly on the use of force, and border controls, may develop where a state does not have sufficient resources to extend its reach to remote regions or to challenge powerful nonstate groups.	Ungoverned or undergoverned territory, which can be geographical but also includes lines of commerce or other ways of conducting business that are hard to observe, monitor, or regulate	Strength of government military, security, and intelligence forces, including outside security assistance	The presence of a vibrant unofficial or underground banking sector (e.g., hawala, black market peso exchange, padala)	What can the government be expected to accomplish with its military and security services?	There is strong agreement in the literature that ungoverned territory frequently serves to perpetuate insurgencies and terrorist groups.	Somalia, Latin American, and African civil wars in 1900s; separatists in Yemen; drug trafficking groups on the Guatemalan-Mexican frontier; Egyptian Islamic Group in central Egypt in the 1990s; Islamic militants in the Indonesian province of Central Sulawesi in the late 1990s
				Difficulty of monitoring land and water borders	The presence of unofficial or unregulated communications infrastructure (e.g., very small aperture terminal [VSAT] or shortwave radio prevalence)	How are insurgents exploiting open land and water borders to move illicit goods, people, and weapons?		
				Availability of exploitable natural resources, such as timber, diamonds, and oil	Government military and security forces are weak and co-opted by politicians, political groups, or armed groups.	How are insurgents exploiting natural resources, such as timber, diamonds, and oil? How might their dependence on these resources be leveraged to undermine their operations?		
				Extent of exploitable communications and transportation infrastructure	Extreme terrain difficulty that reduces government mobility	To what extent do insurgents rely on exploitable communications and transportation infrastructure? How might their use of this infrastructure be disrupted?		

Table B.1—continued

Factor Number	Factor	Key Aspects	Brief Description	Mitigating/ Exacerbating Variables	Metrics and Data Sources	Analytic Questions	Level of Consensus About Salience of Factor	Conflict Examples
7	Multiple armed groups competing for power and influence	Competing, violent groups may have tribal, ethnic, social, or political roots and are more likely to develop in places where the government is unable or unwilling to curtail their activities. Competing groups may also co-evolve their violent tactics and capabilities as they learn from targeting and evading one another.	Many competing armed tribal, social, or political groups pursuing their own agendas and competing for power and influence, which produces an "un-united" front that is difficult to monitor, target, and negotiate with. Additionally, competing groups co-evolve in terms of tactics and capabilities as they learn from targeting one another.	The number of competing armed groups	The presence of multiple small-scale conflicts or multiple armed groups with separate command-and-control, recruiting, and media structures	How many distinct or quasi-distinct armed groups are involved in violent operations?	There is moderate agreement in the literature for this factor, although political scientists have devoted significantly more attention directly to this issue than sociologists and anthropologists have.	Iraq, Afghanistan, Latin American, and African civil wars in 1900s; drug traffickers in northern Mexico; militants in the Federally Administered Tribal Areas (FATA) in Pakistan; drug trafficking and insurgent groups in Colombia in the 1990s; terrorist and criminal groups in Northern Ireland in the 1980s
				The extent to which the armed groups are in violent conflict with one another	Evidence of media operations reflecting divergent and competing agendas. Attacks on one armed group by another.	Which and how many armed groups are in conflict with one another?		

Table B.1—continued

Factor Number	Factor	Key Aspects	Brief Description	Mitigating/ Exacerbating Variables	Metrics and Data Sources	Analytic Questions	Level of Consensus About Salience of Factor	Conflict Examples
7 (cont.)				The capabilities and intentions of each of the armed groups	The presence of armed groups engaging in operations of varying quality. Evidence that groups are evolving as they learn, both cooperatively and competitively, from each other.	What are the operational capabilities and military and political objectives of the various armed groups?		
				The extent to which the armed groups have centers of gravity that can be attacked or disrupted	Armed group attacks are coordinated and choreographed. Resources and intelligence are shared among groups.	Do the armed groups have a collective center of gravity or informal command structure that can be attacked or monitored?		

Table B.1—continued

Factor Number	Factor	Key Aspects	Brief Description	Mitigating/ Exacerbating Variables	Metrics and Data Sources	Analytic Questions	Level of Consensus About Salience of Factor	Conflict Examples
8	Extent to which government allows political or ideological dissent; extent to which individuals feel alienated from governing process	Individuals who are disappointed that they are not able to participate fully in political life and recognize political inequalities (such as those with higher incomes or young people with high education levels) are more likely than their less advantaged counterparts to become involved in a process of radicalization moving toward violence. The key to this factor is the perceived injustices or inequities, with violence being a response to oppression and exploitation.	Disappointed with political life, individuals who are knowledgeable about the gaps between ideals and the realities and who see themselves as significant participants in political struggles	Level of economic inequality in the nation	Gini coefficient: measurement of income inequality	What type of political system does the country have? How does the government handle political grievances?	There is strong disagreement in the social science fields about the relationship between open political participation (democracy) and insurgency. One reason for this is that while there are ample examples in which political oppression has led to violent uprisings, there are also examples worldwide in which a lack of access to political operations or institutionalized barriers to political participation has not led to insurgency.	United States (Weather Underground), al Qaeda network, Colombia in 1960s (FARC)
				Openness of access to education system within country (gross and net education, literacy rates, educational attainment by cohorts)	Extent to which political freedoms are provided by central state government	Does the country hold elections? How free and open/democratic are the elections?		

Table B.1—continued

Factor Number	Factor	Key Aspects	Brief Description	Mitigating/ Exacerbating Variables	Metrics and Data Sources	Analytic Questions	Level of Consensus About Salience of Factor	Conflict Examples
8 (cont.)				Level of oppression, which could determine the level of risk for an insurgency	Extent to which population perceives the political system as fair and open	How many political parties are there?		

Table B.1—continued

Factor Number	Factor	Key Aspects	Brief Description	Mitigating/ Exacerbating Variables	Metrics and Data Sources	Analytic Questions	Level of Consensus About Salience of Factor	Conflict Examples
9	Level of consistency/agreement between insurgent group's goals and philosophy and preferences/worldview/ideology of target populations	This factor refers to the ability of insurgent, terrorist, and other nonstate groups to develop symbols, narratives, and an overall appeal that accords with the local population's sense of identity, morality, and general understanding of the world. This capacity is essential for the recruitment of support and personnel and helps such groups win strategic battles both within their area of operations and with external supporters.	Extent to which the insurgent group has popular support allowing it to recruit, control, deploy, and navigate the area of operations	Economic, financial, and political resources to support insurgent group; Strength and appeal of counternarrative produced by opposing forces; Presence of strong insurgent/terrorist leadership adept at creating compelling narratives of resistance and sacrifice that exploit popular grievances against the ruling elites; Factionalization of ruling elites, loyalty of core constituencies and patronage networks; Presence of extreme in-group/out-group fault lines in the population (ethnic, religious, tribal, etc.)	The presence of insurgent media campaigns that emphasis solidarity with existing ruling or political population; Polling among the local population shows favorable ratings of insurgent group; The presence of deep social, familial, or tribal ties between key elements of the population and key members of the insurgency; High levels of financial and recruiting support in the local population	Does the insurgent group have extensive (and successful) "public outreach" or media operations directed at the population?; What social, familial, or tribal ties exist between the local population and the insurgent group?; What is the local population's private and public sentiment toward the insurgent group?; Is the insurgent group able to raise money and recruit from the local population?	There is strong agreement in the literature regarding the importance of insurgent or other nonstate actors' connection with the cultural sensibilities of the local population to recruit foot soldiers and maintain material and other support. There is active disagreement in the field about the importance of a radical and violent religious ideology (versus other ideological manifestations).	Al Qaeda, Taliban, Mexican civil war (1900s), Northern Ireland (Provisional Irish Republican Army, 1970s), Somali piracy

Table B.1—continued

Factor Number	Factor	Key Aspects	Brief Description	Mitigating/ Exacerbating Variables	Metrics and Data Sources	Analytic Questions	Level of Consensus About Salience of Factor	Conflict Examples
10	Extent to which population and insurgent/ terrorist groups perceive faltering government commitment to COIN campaign	The perception of level of resolve or commitment by local government and external supporters (e.g., another country or global entity, such as NATO) for pursuing a long-term, focused campaign against insurgent groups can affect local cost-benefit analyses of whom to support.	Perception of level of resolve or commitment by government and supporters (e.g., United States)	Population's access to media (or other information) that conveys the level of COIN actor resolve or commitment

The accuracy and credibility of the media to which the population has access

The elasticity of the insurgent's perception of the COIN actor's level of resolve | The presence of multiple media and other information outlets to which the insurgents and the local population have easy access

The presence of media reporting on the COIN actor's resolve that is considered credible by the insurgents | Media descriptions of level of resolve of U.S. involvement in COIN and of the country's government | There is generally strong agreement in the literature about the importance of demonstrating resolve to COIN and counterterrorism | Vietnam War, Iraq, global jihadists |

Table B.1—continued

Factor Number	Factor	Key Aspects	Brief Description	Mitigating/ Exacerbating Variables	Metrics and Data Sources	Analytic Questions	Level of Consensus About Salience of Factor	Conflict Examples
11	Capacity, resources, and expertise of insurgent/ terrorist groups	A group's capacity includes its financial and human capital, technical skills and expertise, ability to adapt, ability to connect with the local population for recruitment and support, resilience to attack, and counter-intelligence capabilities.	How well endowed a group is in terms of • financial and human capital • flexible, distributed organizational dynamics • technical skills and ability to adapt • ability to connect with local population for recruitment and support purposes (including successful use of local cultural themes in messaging and dissemination through popular local media—to include Facebook, Twitter, etc., in contexts where appropriate or via radio, word of mouth, etc.) • resilience to attack (ability to continue presence or influence after heavy bombardment or losses) • ability to hide (either physically or "hiding in plain sight" through blending in)	Influenced to large extent by status of other factors—external support from neighboring states and diasporas, confluence with local worldviews and philosophies/ ideologies, materiel/ intelligence support from locals, etc. Affected by government/ supporter ability to infiltrate, counter presence, establish rule of law and services, and cut off or interrupt means of support	• Insurgent accounting books • Data on external donations • Sophistication and quantity of insurgent IEDs and weaponry, radios and comms, vehicles (gained through seizure, interrogation, ISR imagery, etc.) • Sophistication (complexity, timing, organization) of insurgent operations • Insurgent intelligence collection and counterintelligence capability, reflected by failed operations or infiltration, seized or intercepted enemy intelligence, etc.	What resource endowments were available to groups in the early stages of insurgency? How quickly does a group adapt to changes in COIN strategy and tactics? How well does the group connect with locals in terms of messaging content, worldview overlap, and means of reaching the local population?	There is relatively strong agreement in the literature about the importance of this factor among sociologists and political scientists.	Peru (Shining Path), Uganda (National Resistance Army), Mozambique (Renamo), Haqqani Taliban in Afghanistan, Los Zetas in Mexico, Abu Sayyaf in the Philippines, the Libyan Islamic Fighting Group (LIFG) in the Sahel region

Table B.1—continued

Factor Number	Factor	Key Aspects	Brief Description	Mitigating/ Exacerbating Variables	Metrics and Data Sources	Analytic Questions	Level of Consensus About Salience of Factor	Conflict Examples
11 (cont.)					• Sophistication and effectiveness of insurgent messaging (themes and media) and other outreach (e.g., recruitment) • Effectiveness or failure of modeling or other techniques to predict enemy activity • Govt./supporter ability to track/monitor insurgents and distinguish insurgents from population • Observed ability of insurgent group to change behaviors in response to attacks			

Table B.1—continued

Factor Number	Factor	Key Aspects	Brief Description	Mitigating/ Exacerbating Variables	Metrics and Data Sources	Analytic Questions	Level of Consensus About Salience of Factor	Conflict Examples
12	Social networks capable of being galvanized and mobilized to resistant action	Violent, nonstate actors leverage traditional and virtual social networks to connect, recruit, induce "self-radicalization," and propagate their ideologies, including international outreach for support and homegrown IO.	Social networks, including those connected through family, tribe, ethnicity, and other group dynamics. More recently, use of social media (Facebook, Twitter, text messaging, chat rooms, message boards, etc.).	Fragmentation or split loyalties of groups Significant group or subgroup differences in modes of communication State monitoring of and control of access to communication technologies and other modes of communication (as well as popular perception of the state's ability to monitor communication among group's members) Population support or tolerance for radical or violent political messages and networking	Social networking/ media and communication technology used overtly or covertly to attempt to organize, rally, or recruit violent, nonstate actors Popular support or tolerance for radical messaging as reflected in social media content Detainees report using social media technologies to communicate or otherwise are social media–savvy. Sufficient Internet and/or cellular network penetration in a given region	What kinds of traditional networks exist, and how are they used in recruitment, planning, and dissemination? Is there widespread support for or rejection of violent ideologies and actions? What are the major ideological streams? Where are the state's gaps in controlling, monitoring, and analyzing the content of communications mediums?	There is strong agreement within the social science fields about the importance of the use of social networks in supporting insurgencies or conflict. However, there is strong disagreement within the literature and among our expert interviewees about the extent to which social media, in connecting and mobilizing popular resistance and civil disobedience, spurs violent action.	Syria, Egypt (Arab Spring protestors/ militants, 2011); Zapatistas (Mexico, 1994)

NOTES: AQAP = Al Qaeda in the Arabian Peninsula; IED = improvised explosive device; ISR = intelligence, surveillance, and reconnaissance; OIF = Operation Iraqi Freedom.

Cross-Matching 12 Factors with RAND Case Studies on 30 Counterinsurgencies

As part of our effort to corroborate the factors that we identified as instigators or perpetuators of unstable environments that are susceptible to insurgency and terrorism, we cross-matched our 12 factors against 75 factors used in *Victory Has a Thousand Fathers: Detailed Counterinsurgency Case Studies*, a study of 30 counterinsurgency cases led by RAND colleague Christopher Paul.[1] Table C.1 displays the results of this cross-matching and identifies which of our 12 factors were present in each insurgency. The cross-matching methodology is described below.

Methodology for *Thousand Fathers* Case Study Cross-Matching

The first step was to create a cross-walk between the 12 factors we identified and the factors coded as predictors of COIN wins and losses in Paul, Clarke, and Grill's work ("COIN factors"). Of our 12 factors, we found that seven had multiple matching COIN factors that were explicitly coded in *Victory Has a Thousand Fathers*—Factors 1, 2, 5, 6, 8, 10, and 11. In some cases, the COIN factors were the inverse of our factor. For example, Factor 1 (external support for violent, nonstate groups) matched with Paul, Clarke, and Grill's COIN factors of "important external support to insurgents significantly reduced" and "external support to insurgents from strong state/military." Also, Factors 5 and 6 shared matching COIN factors with each other ("government provided better governance than insurgents in area of conflict" and "insurgents provided or ensured basic services in areas they controlled or claimed"). The 12 factors and matching COIN factors are listed below.

Paul, Clarke, and Grill's work provided a list of all factors that factored into COIN wins and losses for up to four individual stages of 30 different COIN conflicts throughout history. We coded all of the pertinent COIN factors and then color-coded them to determine which of our factors were associated with each of the 30 COIN conflicts. To cover our remaining five factors that had no matching COIN factors, and to ensure that we had covered the available evidence, we then read through all of the narrative case studies and hand-coded evidence for each of our factors in each conflict. We found that a number of our remaining factors were described in the text of the case studies but were not included as part of the 75 COIN factors. This provided a final count of conflicts with evidence for each of our factors.

---

[1]   Paul, Clarke, and Grill, 2010.

Table C.1
Presence of Factors in 30 Case Studies

Factor	DRC (Anti-Kabila)	Nepal	Kosovo	Zaire (Anti-Mobutu)	Afghanistan (Taliban)	Chechnya	Burundi	Bosnia Phase I (1992)	Nagorno-Karabakh	Georgia/Abkhazia	Tajikistan	Afghanistan (Post-Soviet)	Croatia	Algeria (GIA)	Sierra Leone	Moldova	Rwanda	Liberia	Papua New Guinea	Uganda (ADF)	Sudan	Turkey (PKK)	Senegal	Nicaragua (Contras)	Peru	Somalia	El Salvador	Kampuchea	Afghanistan (Anti-Soviet)	Nicaragua (Somoza)
1. External support	×		×	×	×		×	×	×	×	×	×	×	×	×	×	×	×	×	×	×	×	×	×			×	×	×	×
2. Government considered illegitimate/ineffective		×		×			×			×	×	×		×	×			×					×		×		×	×	×	×
3. History of resisting state rule					×						×	×		×					×							×			×	
4. Poverty/inequality							×												×						×					
5. Local governance fragmented/weak				×	×						×	×			×	×					×	×			×	×			×	
6. Ungoverned space	×														×						×		×							
7. Multiple armed groups							×	×	×		×	×					×			×	×					×				
8. Oppression/repression/alienation												×													×	×				
9. Consistency/agreement between insurgents and population					×							×				×			×	×	×	×		×	×	×	×		×	
10. Faltering commitment to campaign																		×	×											
11. Capacity of insurgent/terrorist group		×		×		×		×	×			×				×	×			×	×	×		×	×	×	×		×	×
12. Social networks					×																									

NOTES: ADF = Allied Democratic Forces, GIA = Armed Islamic Group, PKK = Kurdistan Workers' Party.

Twelve factors with matching COIN factors ("inverse" COIN factors noted in *italics*):

Factor 1: External support for violent, nonstate groups
- Important external support to insurgents significantly reduced
- External support to insurgents from strong state/military
- External professional military engaged in fighting on behalf of insurgents

Factor 2: Government considered illegitimate and ineffective by the population
- *Short-term investments, improvements in infrastructure/development, or property reform in area of conflict controlled or claimed by COIN force*
- *Government corruption reduced/good governance increased since onset of conflict*
- *COIN force provided or ensured provision of basic services in areas it controlled or claimed to control*
- *Majority of citizens in area of conflict viewed government as legitimate*
- *Insurgents discredited/delegitimized COIN force/government*
- *Government/state was competent*

Factor 3: Tribal or ethnic indigenous populations with history of resisting state rule, and/or cultures that encourage or justify violent behavior

Factor 4: Absolute or relative poverty/inequality, presence of one or more groups that have recently lost status or power

Factor 5: Local governance fragmented or nonexistent and vulnerable to co-option from insurgent replacement institutions
- *Government provided better governance than insurgents in area of conflict*
- Insurgents provided or ensured basic services in areas they controlled or claimed

Factor 6: Ungoverned space
- *Government provided better governance than insurgents in area of conflict*
- Insurgents provided or ensured basic services in areas they controlled or claimed
- Expropriable cash crops or mineral wealth in area of conflict

Factor 7: Multiple violent, nonstate groups competing for power

Factor 8: Government does not allow for political or ideological dissent; individuals feel alienated from governing process
- *Government leaders selected in a manner considered just and fair by majority of population in area of conflict*
- *Government a functional democracy*
- *Government a partial or transitional democracy*
- *Free and fair elections held*
- *Government respected human rights and allowed free press*

Factor 9: Level of consistency/agreement between insurgent group's goals and philosophy and preferences/worldview/ideology of target populations

Factor 10: Population and insurgent/terrorist groups perceive faltering government commitment to COIN campaign
- *Unity of effort/unity of command maintained*
- *COIN force and government had different goals/levels of commitment*

Factor 11: Capacity, resources, and expertise of violent, nonstate groups
- *COIN force effectively disrupted insurgent recruiting*
- *COIN force effectively disrupted insurgent materiel acquisition*
- *COIN force effectively disrupted insurgent intelligence*
- *COIN force effectively disrupted insurgent financing*
- *COIN force effectively disrupted insurgent command and control*
- *Flow of cross-border insurgent support significantly decreased in this phase or remained dramatically reduced or absent*
- *Important internal support to insurgents significantly reduced*
- *Insurgents unable to maintain or grow force size*
- *Insurgents' ability to replenish resources significantly diminished*

Factor 12: Social networks capable of being galvanized and mobilized to resistant action.

Bibliography

12th Air Force, "Medical Readiness Training Exercises (MEDRETEs)," factsheet, June 2008. As of June 19, 2012:
http://www.12af.acc.af.mil/library/factsheets/factsheet.asp?id=7694

Abbott, Andrew, "Conceptions of Time and Events in Social Science Methods: Causal and Narrative Approaches," *Historical Methods*, Vol. 23, No. 4, 1990, pp. 140–150.

Allen, L., "Getting by the Occupation: How Violence Became Normal During the Second Palestinian Intifada," *Cultural Anthropology*, Vol. 23, No. 3, 2008, pp. 453–487.

Aminzade, Ronald, "Historical Sociology and Time," *Sociological Methods & Research*, Vol. 20, No. 4, 1992, p. 463.

Arquilla, John, and David Ronfeldt, *The Advent of Netwar,* Santa Monica, Calif.: RAND Corporation, MR-789-OSD, 1996. As of June 19, 2012:
http://www.rand.org/pubs/monograph_reports/MR789.html

Arquilla, John, and David Ronfeldt, eds., *Networks and Netwars: The Future of Terror, Crime, and Militancy,* Santa Monica, Calif.: RAND Corporation, MR-1382-OSD, 2001. As June 19, 2012:
http://www.rand.org/pubs/monograph_reports/MR1382.html

Atzili, Boaz, "State Weakness and 'Vacuum of Power' in Lebanon," *Terrorism*, Vol. 33, No. 8, 2010, pp. 757–782. As of February 7, 2012:
http://www.tandfonline.com/doi/pdf/10.1080/1057610X.2010.494172

Austin, Roy L., "Adolescent Subcultures of Violence," *The Sociological Quarterly*, Vol. 21, No. 4, 1980, pp. 545–561. As of July 2, 2012:
http://www.jstor.org/discover/10.2307/
4106138?uid=3739560&uid=2129&uid=2&uid=70&uid=4&uid=3739256&sid=21100892574201

Ayoob, Mohammed, "The Future of Political Islam: The Importance of External Variables," *International Affairs,* Vol. 81, No. 5, 2005, pp. 951–961.

Ayres, Jeffrey M., "Framing Collective Action Against Neoliberalism: The Case of the Anti-Globalization Movement," *Journal of World-Systems Research*, Vol. 10, No. 1, 2004, pp. 10–34.

Ayres, Jeffrey M., "From the Streets to the Internet," *Annals of the American Academy of Political and Social Science*, Vol. 566, 1999, pp. 132–143.

Ballentine, Karen, and Jake Sherman, eds., *The Political Economy of Armed Conflict: Beyond Greed and Grievance*, Boulder, Colo.: Lynne Rienner Publishers, 2003.

Barfield, T., "Culture and Custom in Nation-Building: Law in Afghanistan," *Maine Law Review*, Vol. 60, No. 2, 2008.

Beck, Colin, "The Contribution of Social Movement Theory to Understanding Terrorism," *Sociology Compass*, Vol. 2, No. 5, 2008, pp. 1565–1581.

Bendle, Mervyn F., "Militant Religion and the Crisis of Modernity: A New Paradigm," *Research in the Social Scientific Study of Religion*, Vol. 14, 2003, pp. 229–252.

Benford, Robert D., and David A. Snow, "Framing Processes and Social Movements: An Overview and Assessment," *Annual Review of Sociology,* Vol. 26, 2000, pp. 611–639.

Bennett, W. Lance, "Communicating Global Activism," *Information, Communication & Society*, Vol. 6, No. 2, 2003a, pp. 143–168.

Bennett, W. Lance, "New Media Power," in Nick Couldry and James Curran, eds., *Contesting Media Power*, Lanham, Md.: Rowman & Littlefield, 2003b.

Berdal, Mats R., and David Malone, *Greed and Grievance: Economic Agendas in Civil Wars*, Boulder, Colo.: Lynne Rienner Publishers, 2000.

Berman, Eli, Michael Callen, Joseph H. Felter, and Jacob N. Shapiro, *Do Working Men Rebel? Insurgency and Unemployment in Iraq and the Philippines*, Cambridge, Mass.: National Bureau of Economic Research, Working Paper 15547, November 2009. As of June 19, 2012:
http://www.nber.org/papers/w15547.pdf

Binford, Leigh, "Violence in El Salvador," *Ethnography*, Vol. 3, No. 2, 2002, pp. 201–219.

Bourgois, P., "In Search of Masculinity: Violence, Respect and Sexuality Among Puerto Rican Crack Dealers in East Harlem," *British Journal of Criminology*, Vol. 36, No. 3, 1996, pp. 412–427.

Bourgois, P., "The Power of Violence in War and Peace," *Ethnography*, Vol. 2, No. 1, 2001, pp. 5–34.

Byman, Daniel, *Deadly Connections: States That Sponsor Terrorism*, New York: Cambridge University Press, 2005.

Byman, Daniel, *Understanding Proto-Insurgencies*, Santa Monica, Calif.: RAND Corporation, OP-178-OSD, 2007. As of September 17, 2013:
http://www.rand.org/pubs/occasional_papers/OP178.html

Byman, Daniel, Peter Chalk, Bruce Hoffman, William Rosenau, and David Brannan, *Trends in Outside Support for Insurgent Movements*, Santa Monica, Calif.: RAND Corporation, MR-1405-OTI, 2001. As of June 19, 2012:
http://www.rand.org/pubs/monograph_reports/MR1405.html

Carley, Kathleen M., "Destabilization of Covert Networks," *Computational & Mathematical Organization Theory*, Vol. 12, No. 1, 2006, pp. 51–66. As of June 27, 2012:
http://dl.acm.org/citation.cfm?id=1132099.1132105

Castells, Manuel, *The Rise of the Network Society*, Oxford, UK: Blackwell Publishers, 1996.

Castells, Manuel, *The Power of Identity (The Information Age: Economy, Society and Culture, Volume II)*, Oxford, UK: Blackwell Publishers, 1997.

Castells, Manuel, *The Network Society: A Cross-Cultural Perspective*, London, UK: Edward Elgar, 2004.

Center for Army Lessons Learned, *Newsletter 11-34: Irregular Warfare: A SOF Perspective*, June 2011.

Chagnon, N. A., "Life Histories, Blood Revenge, and Warfare in a Tribal Population," *Science*, Vol. 239, No. 4843, 1988, pp. 985–992.

Chisholm, J. S., *Death, Hope and Sex: Steps to an Evolutionary Ecology of Mind and Morality*, New York: Cambridge University Press, 1999.

Cleaver, Harry, *The Zapatistas and the Electronic Fabric of Struggle*, Web version, 1995. As of February 7, 2012:
http://www.eco.utexas.edu/faculty/Cleaver/zaps.html

Cleaver, Harry, *Computer-Linked Social Movements and the Threat to Global Capitalism*, Web version, 1999. As of February 7, 2012:
http://www.eco.utexas.edu/faculty/Cleaver/polnet.html

Coleman, James, *Foundations of Social Theory*, Cambridge, UK: Belknap, 1990.

Collier, Paul, and Anke Hoeffler, "On Economic Causes of Civil War," *Oxford Economic Papers*, Vol. 50, No. 4, 1998, pp. 563–573.

Collier, Paul, and Anke Hoeffler, "Greed and Grievance in Civil War," *The Centre for the Study of African Economies Working Paper Series*, Working Paper 160, July 1, 2002.

Collins, Randall, *Conflict Sociology: Toward an Explanatory Science,* New York: Academic Press, 1975.

Collins, Randall, *Four Sociological Traditions: Selected Readings*, Oxford, UK: Oxford University Press, 1994.

Commission on Truth and Reconciliation (Comisión de la Verdad y Reconciliación), Vol. VI, Chapter 1, August 23, 2003, p. 41. As of May 11, 2012:
http://www.usip.org/files/file/resources/collections/commissions/Peru01-Report/Peru01-Report_Vol6.pdf

Compton, J. Bernhard, "Violent Non-State Actors in the Middle Eastern Region," *Small Wars Journal*, 2008. As of February 7, 2012:
http://smallwarsjournal.com/blog/journal/docs-temp/88-compton.pdf?q=mag/docs-temp/88-compton.pdf

Connable, Ben, *Embracing the Fog of War: Assessment and Metrics in Counterinsurgency*, Santa Monica, Calif.: RAND Corporation, MG-1086-DOD, 2012. As of June 19, 2012:
http://www.rand.org/pubs/monographs/MG1086.html

Connable, Ben, and Martin Libicki, *How Insurgencies End*, Santa Monica, Calif.: RAND Corporation, MG-965-MCIA, 2010. As of December 2012:
http://www.rand.org/pubs/monographs/MG965

Council on Foreign Relations, "Backgrounder: Hamas," Web page, October 20, 2011. As of May 17, 2012:
http://www.cfr.org/israel/hamas/p8968

Crenshaw, Martha, "The Causes of Terrorism," *Comparative Politics*, Vol. 13, No. 4, 1981.

Daly, M., M. Wilson, and S. Vasdev, "Income Inequality and Homicide Rates in Canada and the United States," *Canadian Journal of Criminology*, Vol. 43, No. 2, 2001, pp. 219–236.

Davis, Paul K., and Kim Cragin, eds., *Social Science for Counterterrorism: Putting the Pieces Together*, Santa Monica, Calif.: RAND Corporation, MG-849-OSD, 2009. As of June 25, 2012:
http://www.rand.org/pubs/monographs/MG849.html

Farley, Jonathan David, "Breaking al Qaeda Cells: A Mathematical Analysis of Counterterrorism Operations (A Guide for Risk Assessment and Decision Making)," *Studies in Conflict & Terrorism*, Vol. 26, 2003, pp. 399–411.

Fearon, James, "Rationalist Explanations for War," *International Organization*, Vol. 49, No. 3, 1995, pp. 379–414.

Fearon, James, and David Laitin, "Ethnicity, Insurgency, and Civil War," *American Political Science Review*, Vol. 97, No. 1, February 2003.

Fettweis, Christopher, "America's Dangerous Obsession: Credibility and the War on Terror," *Political Science Quarterly,* Vol. 122, No. 4, 2007–2008, pp. 607–633.

Fry, D. P., "'Respect for the Rights of Others Is Peace': Learning Aggression Versus Nonaggression Among the Zapotec," *American Anthropologist*, Vol. 94, No. 3, 1992, pp. 621–639.

Gamson, William A., *The Strategy of Social Protest*, Homewood, Ill.: Dorsey Press, 1975.

Gamson, William A., *Talking Politics*, New York: Cambridge University Press, 1992.

Ganor, Boaz, *The Counter-Terrorism Puzzle*, New Brunswick, N.J.: Transaction Publishers, 2005.

Gould, Roger V., "Multiple Networks and Mobilization in the Paris Commune, 1871," *American Sociological Review*, Vol. 56, No. 6, 1991, pp. 716–729.

Granovetter, Mark, "The Strength of Weak Ties," *The American Journal of Sociology*, Vol. 78, No. 6, 1973, pp. 1360–1380.

Granovetter, Mark, "The Strength of Weak Ties: A Network Theory Revisited," in P. V. Marsden and N. Lin, eds., *Social Structure and Network Analysis*, Beverly Hills, Calif.: Sage Publications, 1982, pp. 105–130.

Gregory, Kathryn, "Backgrounder: Shining Path, Tupac Amaru," Web page, Council on Foreign Relations, August 27, 2009. As of May 8, 2012:
http://www.cfr.org/terrorism/shining-path-tupac-amaru-peru-leftists/p9276

Griffith, Kevin, "The People Are the Prize: Social Bonds as a Counterinsurgency Objective," *Phalanx*, December 2010.

Gurr, Ted, *Why Men Rebel,* Princeton, N.J.: Princeton University Press, 1970.

Haas, J. ed., *The Anthropology of War*, Cambridge, UK: Cambridge University Press, 1990.

Hafez, Mohammed M., *Why Muslims Rebel: Repression and Resistance in the Islamic World*, Boulder, Colo.: Lynne Rienner Publishers, 2003

Hammes, T. X., "War Evolves into the Fourth Generation," *Contemporary Security Policy*, Vol. 26, No. 2, 2005, pp. 189–221.

Hanlin, R., "One Team's Approach to VSO," *Small Wars Journal*, Vol. 7, No. 9, 2011, pp. 1–8.

Headquarters, Department of the Army, *Field Manual 3-05.202: Special Forces Foreign Internal Defense Operations*, February 2007.

Headquarters, Department of the Army, *Field Manual 3-0: Operations*, February 2008. As of May 20, 2012: http://www.fas.org/irp/doddir/army/fm3-0.pdf

Headquarters, Department of the Army, *FM 3-24: Counterinsurgency*, December 2006, pp. 21–23.

Herdt, G., "Aspects of Socialization for Aggression in Sambia Ritual and Warfare," *Anthropological Quarterly*, Vol. 59, No. 4, 1986, pp. 160–164.

Hirschi, Travis, *Causes of Delinquency*, New Brunswick, N.J.: Transaction Publishers, 2002.

Hsieh, C., and M. D. Pugh, "Poverty, Income Inequality, and Violent Crime: A Meta-Analysis of Recent Aggregate Data Studies," *Criminal Justice Review*, Vol. 18, No. 2, 1993, pp. 182–202.

Hudson, Rex A., ed., *Peru: A Country Study*, Library of Congress, Washington, D.C.: Government Printing Office, 1992. As of May 11, 2012: http://countrystudies.us/peru/48.htm

Human Rights Watch, *Leave None to Tell the Story*, HRW Legacy Reports, 1999.

Huntington, S. P., *The Clash of Civilizations and the Remaking of World Order*, New York: Simon & Schuster, 1996.

Iyengar, Radha, and Jonathan Monten, "Is There an 'Emboldenment' Effect? Evidence from the Insurgency in Iraq," NBER Working Paper No. 13839, May 2008.

Jenkins, J. Craig, "Resource Mobilization Theory and the Study of Social Movements," *Annual Review of Sociology*, Vol. 9, 1983, pp. 527–553.

Johnston, H., "Ritual, Strategy, and Deep Culture in the Chechen National Movement," *Critical Studies on Terrorism*, Vol. 1, No. 3, 2008, pp. 321–342.

Juergensmeyer, Mark, *Terror in the Mind of God: The Global Rise of Religious Violence*, Berkeley, Calif.: University of California Press, 2003.

Juris, Jeffrey S., "The New Media and Activist Networking within Anti-Corporate Globalization Movements," *Annals of the American Academy of Political and Social Science,* Vol. 597, No. 1, 2005, pp. 189–208.

Katz, David, "Reforming the Village War," *Middle East Quarterly*, Spring 2011, pp. 17–31.

Keiser, Lincoln, *Friend by Day, Enemy by Night: Organized Vengeance in a Kohistani Community*, Fort Worth, Tex.: Holt, Rinehart, and Winston, 1991.

Keiser, R. Lincoln, "Death Enmity in Thull: Organized Vengeance and Social Change in a Kohistani Community," *American Ethnologist*, Vol. 13, No. 3, 1986, pp. 489–505.

Kilcullen, David, *The Accidental Guerilla: Fighting Small Wars in the Midst of a Big One*, New York: Oxford University Press, 2009.

Kilcullen, David, *Counterinsurgency*, New York: Oxford University Press, 2010.

Kimmage, Daniel, and Kathleen Ridolfo, "Iraq's Networked Insurgents," *Foreign Policy,* October 11, 2007. As of July 1, 2012: http://www.foreignpolicy.com/articles/2007/10/11/iraqs_networked_insurgents

Klein, Malcolm W., *The American Street Gang: Its Nature, Prevalence, and Control*, Oxford, UK: Oxford University Press, 1995.

Kornhauser, William, *The Politics of Mass Society*, Glencoe, Ill.: The Free Press of Glencoe, 1959.

Krueger, A. B., and J. Maleckova, *Education, Poverty, Political Violence, and Terrorism: Is There a Causal Connection?* Cambridge, Mass.: National Bureau of Economic Research Working Papers, 2002.

Krueger, Alan B., and Jitka Maleckova, "Education, Poverty and Terrorism: Is There a Causal Connection?" *Journal of Economic Perspectives*, Vol. 17, No. 4, Fall 2003, pp. 119–144.

Kruglanski, A. W., and S. Fishman, "The Psychology of Terrorism: 'Syndrome' Versus 'Tool' Perspectives," *Terrorism and Political Violence*, Vol. 18, No. 2, 2006, pp. 193–215.

Kurzman, Charles, "Structural Opportunity and Perceived Opportunity in Social-Movement Theory: The Iranian Revolution of 1979," *American Sociological Review*, Vol. 61, No. 1, pp. 153–170.

Kurzman, Charles, *The Unthinkable Revolution in Iran*, Cambridge, Mass.: Harvard University Press, 2004.

Lamb, Robert D., "Ungoverned Areas and Threats from Safe Havens," Washington, D.C.: Office of the Under Secretary of Defense for Policy, DTIC Document ADA479805, 2008. As of December 2012: http://www.dtic.mil/cgi-bin/GetTRDoc?Location=U2&doc=GetTRDoc.pdf&AD=ADA479805

Lamborn, G. L., *Arms of Little Value: The Challenge of Insurgency and Global Instability in the Twenty-First Century*, Philadelphia, Pa.: Casemate Publishers, 2012.

Lilly, J. Robert, Francis T. Cullen, and Richard A. Ball, *Criminology Theory: Context and Consequences*, Thousand Oaks, Calif.: Sage Publications, 2007.

Love, M. J. B., *Hezbollah: A Charitable Revolution*, School of Advanced Military Studies Monographs, Fort Leavenworth, Kan.: U.S. Army School of Advanced Military Studies, 2008.

Marchal, R., "Somali Piracy: The Local Contexts of an International Obsession," *Humanity*, Spring 2011, pp. 31–50.

Marsden, Peter, "Core Discussion Networks of Americans," *American Sociological Review*, Vol. 52, No. 1, 1987, pp. 122–131.

Marx, Gary T. and James L. Wood, "Strands of Theory and Research in Collective Behavior," *Annual Review of Sociology*, Vol. 1, 1975, pp. 363–428.

Mazarr, Michael J., "The Psychological Sources of Islamic Terrorism: Alienation and Identity in the Arab World," *Hoover.org/Policy Review*, No. 125, Stanford University, June 1, 2004. As of June 1, 2004: http://www.hoover.org/publications/policy-review/article/6864

McAdam, Doug, *Political Process and the Development of Black Insurgency, 1930–1970*, Chicago, Ill.: University of Chicago Press, 1982.

McAdam, Doug, "Tactical Innovation and the Pace of Insurgency," *American Sociological Review*, Vol. 48, No. 6, 1983, pp. 735–754.

McAdam, Doug, John D. McCarthy, and Mayer N. Zald, eds., *Comparative Perspectives on Social Movements: Political Opportunities, Mobilizing Structures, and Cultural Framings*, Cambridge, UK: Cambridge University Press, 1996.

McAdam, Doug, and Ronnelle Paulsen, "Specifying the Relationship Between Social Ties and Activism," *American Journal of Sociology*, Vol. 99, No. 3, 1993, pp. 640–667.

McAdam, Doug, Sidney Tarrow, and Charles Tilly, "To Map Contentious Politics," *Mobilization*, Vol. 1, 1996, pp. 17–34.

McAdam, Doug, Sidney Tarrow, and Charles Tilly, *Dynamics of Contention*, Cambridge, UK: Cambridge University Press, 2001.

McCarthy, John D., and Mayer N. Zald, "The Trend of Social Movements in America: Professionalization and Resource Mobilization," Morristown, N.J.: General Learning Press, 1973.

McCarthy, John D., and Mayer N. Zald, "Resource Mobilization and Social Movements: A Partial Theory," Vol. 82, No. 6, May 1977, pp. 1212–1241.

Miller, Daniel, and Don Slater, *The Internet: An Ethnographic Approach*, Oxford, UK: Berg Publishers, 2000.

Mills, C. Wright, *Power, Politics, and People: The Collected Essays of C. Wright Mills,* Oxford, UK: Oxford University Press, 1963.

Monroe, Kristen Renwick, "Psychology and Rational Actor Theory," *Political Psychology*, Vol. 16, No. 1, pp. 1–21.

Moore, Joan, Diego Vigil, and Robert Garcia, "Residence and Territoriality in Chicano Gangs," *Social Problems*, Vol. 31, No. 2, December 1983.

O'Brien, Sean P., "Anticipating the Good, the Bad, and the Ugly: An Early Warning Approach to Conflict and Instability Analysis," *Journal of Conflict Resolution*, Vol. 46, No. 6, December 2002, pp. 791–811.

Olesen, Thomas, *Long Distance Zapatismo*, London, UK: Zed Books, 2004.

Olson, Mancur, *The Logic of Collective Action: Public Goods and the Theory of Groups*, Cambridge, Mass.: Harvard University Press, 1965.

Pape, R. A., and J. K. Feldman, *Cutting the Fuse: The Explosion of Global Suicide Terrorism and How to Stop It*, Chicago, Ill.: University of Chicago Press, 2010.

Pape, Robert, *Dying to Win: The Strategic Logic of Suicide Terrorism*, New York: Random House, 2005.

Paul, Christopher, Colin P. Clarke, and Beth Grill, *Victory Has a Thousand Fathers: Detailed Counterinsurgency Case Studies*, Santa Monica, Calif.: RAND Corporation, MG-964/1-OSD, 2010. As of June 25, 2012: http://www.rand.org/pubs/monographs/MG964z1.html

Paul, Christopher, Russell W. Glenn, Beth Grill, Megan McKernan, Barbara Raymond, Matthew Stafford, and Horacio R. Trujillo, "Identifying Urban Flashpoints: A Delphi Derived Model for Scoring Cities' Vulnerability to Large Scale Unrest," *Studies in Conflict and Terrorism*, Vol. 31, No. 1, 2008.

Pedahzur, Ami, and Arie Perliger, "The Changing Nature of Suicide Attacks: A Social Network Perspective," *Social Forces*, Vol. 84, No. 4, 2006, pp. 1987–2008.

Polletta, Francesca, "'It Was Like a Fever…': Narrative and Identity in Social Protest," *Society for the Study of Social Problems,* Vol. 45, No. 2, 1998, pp. 137–159.

Polletta, Francesca, *It Was Like a Fever: Storytelling in Protest and Politics,* Chicago, Ill.: University of Chicago Press, 2006.

Powell, Walter W., and Paul J. DiMaggio, eds., *The New Institutionalism in Organizational Analysis*, Chicago, Ill.: University of Chicago Press, 1991.

Quillen, Chris, "A Historical Analysis of Mass Casualty Bombers," *Studies in Conflict and Terrorism*, Vol. 25, No. 5, 2002.

Rabasa, Angel, Steven Boraz, Peter Chalk, Kim Cragin, Theodore W. Karasik, Jennifer D. P. Moroney, Kevin A. O'Brien, and John E. Peters, *Ungoverned Territories: Understanding and Reducing Terrorism Risks*, Santa Monica, Calif.: RAND Corporation, MG-561-PAF, 2007. As of June 25, 2012: http://www.rand.org/pubs/monographs/MG561.html

Ronfeldt, David, John Arquilla, Graham E. Fuller, and Melissa Fuller, *The Zapatista "Social Netwar" in Mexico*, Santa Monica, Calif.: RAND Corporation, MR-994-A, 1998. As of June 19, 2012: http://www.rand.org/pubs/monograph_reports/MR994.html

Roy, Olivier, "Afghanistan: Back to Tribalism or on to Lebanon?" *Third World Quarterly*, Vol. 11, No. 4, 1989, pp. 70–82.

Rubin, Barnett R., "Crafting a Constitution for Afghanistan," *Journal of Democracy*, Vol. 15, No. 3, 2004, pp. 5–19.

Sageman, Marc, *Understanding Terror Networks*, Philadelphia, Pa.: University of Pennsylvania Press, 2004.

Sapolsky, R. M., "The Influence of Social Hierarchy on Primate Health," *Science*, Vol. 308, No. 5722, 2005, pp. 648–652.

Scheper-Hughes, N., and P. Bourgois, *Violence in War and Peace: An Anthology*, Malden, Mass.: Blackwell Publishing, 2003.

Schlee, G., *How Enemies Are Made: Towards a Theory of Ethnic and Religious Conflicts*, Berghahn Books, 2008.

Schwedler, Jillian, *Faith in Moderation: Islamist Parties in Jordan and Yemen*, New York: Cambridge University Press, 2006.

Scott, J. C., *Weapons of the Weak: Everyday Forms of Peasant Resistance*, New Haven, Conn.: Yale University Press, 1987.

Scott, J. C., *The Art of Not Being Governed: An Anarchist History of Upland Southeast Asia*, New Haven, Conn.: Yale University Press, 2009.

Scott, John, "Social Network Analysis," *Sociology*, Vol. 22, No. 1, 1988, pp. 109–127.

Scott, John, "Rational Choice Theory," in G. Browning, A. Halcli, and F. Webster, eds., *Understanding Contemporary Society: Theories of the Present*, Thousand Oaks, Calif.: Sage Publications, 2000.

Sears, Alan, *A Good Book, In Theory: A Guide to Theoretical Thinking*, North York: Higher Education University of Toronto Press, 2008.

Shannon, Vaughn P., and Michael Dennis, "Militant Islam and the Futile Fight for Reputation," *Security Studies*, Vol. 16, No. 2, 2007, pp. 287–317.

Simons, Anna, "Democratisation and Ethnic Conflict: The Kin Connection," *Nations and Nationalism*, Vol. 3, No. 2, 1997, pp. 273–289.

Simons, Anna, "War: Back to the Future," *Annual Review of Anthropology*, Vol. 28, 1999, pp. 73–108.

Simons, Anna, and David Tucker, "The Misleading Problem of Failed States: A 'Socio-Geography' of Terrorism in the Post-9/11 Era," *Third World Quarterly*, Vol. 28, No. 2, 2007, pp. 387–401.

Smelser, Neil J., *Theory of Collective Behavior*, Glencoe, Ill.: Free Press of Glencoe, 1963.

Snow, David A., E. Burke Rochford, Jr., Steven K. Worden, and Robert D. Benford, "Frame Alignment Processes, Micromobilization, and Movement Participation," *American Sociological Review*, Vol. 51, No. 4, 1986, pp. 464–481.

Snow, David A., and Scott C. Byrd, "Ideology, Framing Processes, and Islamic Terrorist Movements," *Mobilization*, Vol. 12, No. 1, pp. 119–136.

Snow, David A., Rens Vliegenthart, and Catherine Corrigall-Brown, "Framing the French Riots: A Comparative Study of Frame Variation," *Social Forces*, Vol. 86, No. 2, 2007, 385–415.

Sprinzak, Ehud, "Rational Fanatics," *Foreign Policy*, Vol. 120, 2000, pp. 66–74.

Stern, Jessica, *Terror in the Name of God: Why Religious Militants Kill*, New York: Ecco, 2003.

Stryker, Robin, "Beyond History Versus Theory: Strategic Narrative and Sociological Explanation," *Sociological Methods & Research*, Vol. 24, No. 3, 1996, pp. 304–352.

Tarrow, Sidney, *Power in Movement: Social Movements and Contentious Politics*, Cambridge, UK: Cambridge University Press, 1998.

Tilly, Charles, *Social Movements, 1768–2004*, Boulder, Colo.: Paradigm Publishers, 2004.

Turk, Austin, T., "Sociology of Terrorism," *Annual Review of Sociology*, Vol. 30, No. 1, 2004, pp. 271–286.

Tuzin, D. F., "Ritual Violence Among Ilahita Arapesh: The Dynamics of Moral and Religious Uncertainty," in G. H. Herdt., ed., *Rituals of Manhood: Male Initiation in Papua New Guinea*, Berkeley, Calif.: University of California Press, 1982, pp. 321–355.

U.S. Department of Defense, *Department of Defense Dictionary of Military and Associated Terms*, Joint Publication 1-02, Washington, D.C., November 8, 2010a (as amended through December 15, 2012), p. 151.

U.S. Department of Defense, *Irregular Warfare: Countering Irregular Threats, Joint Operating Concept*, Version 2.0, May 17, 2010b.

U.S. Department of Defense, *Sustaining U.S. Global Leadership: Priorities for 21st Century Defense*, Washington, D.C., January 2012.

Van Aelst, Peter, and Stefaan Walgrave, "New Media, New Movements? The Role of the Internet in Shaping the 'Anti-Globalization' Movement," *Information, Communication & Society*, Vol. 5, No. 4, 2002, pp. 465–493.

Vigil, James Diego, "Urban Violence and Street Gangs," *Annual Review of Anthropology*, Vol. 32, 2003, pp. 225–242.

Vinci, Anthony, "A Conceptual Analysis of Warlords," *Review of African Political Economy*, Vol. 34, No. 112, June 2007.

Wasserman, Stanley, and Katherine Faust, *Social Network Analysis: Methods and Applications (Structural Analysis in the Social Sciences),* Cambridge, UK: Cambridge University Press, 1994.

Weinstein, Jeremy, *Inside Rebellion: The Politics of Insurgent Violence*, Cambridge, UK: Cambridge University Press, 2006.

Wellman, Barry, "Physical Place and Cyberplace," *International Journal of Urban and Regional Research,* Vol. 25, No. 2, 2001, pp. 227–252.

Wellman, Barry, and Caroline Haythornthwaite, eds., *The Internet in Everyday Life,* Malden, Mass.: Blackwell, 2002.

Wilkinson, R. G., I. Kawachi, and B. P. Kennedy, "Mortality, the Social Environment, Crime and Violence," *Sociology of Health & Illness*, Vol. 20, No. 5, 1998, pp. 578–597.

Williams, Phil, *Violent Non-State Actors and National and International Security,* Zurich, Switzerland: International Relations and Security Network, 2008. As of November 19, 2013: http://www.isn.ethz.ch/Digital-Library/Publications/Detail/?id=93880

Williams, Phil, "Illicit Markets, Weak States and Violence: Iraq and Mexico," *Crime, Law and Social Change,* Vol. 52, No. 3, 2009, pp. 323–336.

Wilson, James Q., and Joan Petersilia, eds., *Crime,* San Francisco, Calif.: Institute for Contemporary Studies, 1995.